# *The Rough*
*with*
# *The Smooth*

By the same author

**All Generations**
*(with The Offchurch Group: CIO Publishing 1980)*

**On Course in Contemplation**
*(writings by Robert Coulson selected and edited for
The Fellowship of Contemplative Prayer 1981,1989)*

**Spirit and Life**
The official biography of Robert Coulson
founder of The Fellowship of Contemplative Prayer
*(Churchman Publishing 1987)*
*(Second edition revised & updated: The Fellowship of Contemplative Prayer 2007)*

**Postscript: from the letters of Robert Coulson**
*(selected and edited: The Fellowship of Contemplative Prayer 1994)*

**Exploring Contemplative Prayer**
*(with Peter Dodson: Kevin Mayhew 2005)*

**Ministry Matters: 100 years of ordained ministry
in the Church of England**
*(privately published 2010)*

**Within Thy Silence**
*(compiled and edited: O-Books 2010)*

**The Last of the Bluebells**
*(privately published 2011)*

# *The Rough*
## *with*
# *The Smooth*

random thoughts on
familiar christian themes

MARTIN TUNNICLIFFE

THE CHOIR PRESS

First published in the United Kingdom in 2020 by
The Choir Press

ISBN 978-1-78963-112-8

———◄o►———

## Front cover picture

Faith is a strange thing. We all know what it is, but do we *really* know what it is? Are we born with it, or do we acquire it some time later? Or perhaps we are given it at some point. Can we put it on like a coat when we need it, and take it off again when we don't? Are we stuck with it, or without it?

The cover picture shows part of the inside of Boxgrove Priory near Chichester. I think it illustrates, in part at least, the curious nature of faith. The building is beautiful and has been standing for nine hundred years, stable, familiar, inspiring, a monument to faith, and there are thousands of such buildings of different shapes and sizes all over the planet. On the floor at the back is a maze picked out in tiles, tortuous, enigmatic, an invitation to go on a journey with twists and turns and dead ends, yet with a true centre.

I find these two symbols, the sacred building and the maze, to be an eloquent statement about faith. So they stand as a gentle invitation at the start of this book to come with me for a time along the way of my own faith journey.

# Contents

# Illustrations by the author

# *Foreword*

The Revd. Canon Jane Kenchington
Rector of Solihull

"Random thoughts on familiar Christian themes" is the subtitle of this book. Don't be fooled by it! What Martin has written is wide-ranging, far more than a collection of random thoughts. You will find thought-provoking theological reflections, even a few sermons perhaps, for a seasoned preacher betrays himself. His "random thoughts" encompass Death, the Holiness of God, the Church, unemployment, Christian faith, the problem of suffering, sin, dogs and souls, even psychic fairs.

In this year of 2020, Solihull Churches are celebrating 800 years of Christianity. Martin Tunnicliffe, who has only lived just over one tenth of that time, retired from active ministry in 1998 to live in Solihull Parish. Since then, parishioners have been blessed by having been able to read the many articles that he has written for our monthly Parish News. In this book, he has brought a selection of them together, presented for us to ponder over and to help us draw more closely to God in deeper prayer and faith. His sketches add lighter interludes between the articles.

As we celebrate our 8th centenary, we are aware we inhabit an anxious Church. In the face of numerical decline, we are driven by the "numbers game" as well as feeling pressured by business models of "success", putting on services or events that have to be attractive enough for the consumer culture in which we live. Martin has some firm things to say about this, reminding us of the need to allow Jesus to be enthroned in our hearts, to put our trust and faith totally in God, and that without a contemplative spirituality we are barking up the wrong tree. He challenges the Church to stop becoming a club whose members, anxious about decline, create a Church that focuses mainly on mutual support. By contrast, he reminds us that we are called to be a worshipping centre, a living organism that reflects and radiates the glory of God in a God-lacking society.

Martin challenges us and comforts us. You will find remarks such as "We contend with a God who is as tough as he is tender", "A little reflection reveals that the statement religion and politics don't mix is about as shallow as the Dogger Bank at low tide", "The nearer we are to Jesus Christ, in prayer and action, the more likely we are to get things right."

The second part of the book begins with a reflection on death. Martin quotes Mozart, "death is the true goal of our lives." To many people this is a shocking thing to read. We, who in our current Western society are prepared to spend so much time and money and medical technology trying to extend our lives on earth, are firmly reminded that this earthly life isn't all there is. Christians are meant to sing this Alleluia song because we live an Easter faith. We spend this earthly life preparing for the next stage in our spiritual journey.

Martin Tunnicliffe has the gift of writing in a clear and accessible way. I feel that we are privileged to receive some of the wisdom he has gleaned through his life of prayer, discipleship and ministry.

J.K.

# *Introduction*

During the past twenty years it has been a pleasure for me to continue a kind of ministry by writing articles for the Solihull Parish Magazine.[1] The presentation of this selection is fairly random, so you can open it where you like and read it in bite-size pieces. The chapters in Part Two contain articles that have a vague connection with each other, but you can ignore that if you wish.

It is a salutary exercise to try and see ourselves as others see us. I think that if there is any overriding idea or theme in the articles I write, it would be "to see ourselves as God sees us". Now that puts self-knowledge on a different plane altogether. First of all, it cannot be just an individual exercise: it needs to be collective and connective, bearing in mind that we share a common humanity as we attempt to navigate our individual paths through life. Also, to see yourself as God sees you, you need to have faith, to be active in a faith, and to know something about the sacred scriptures.

You may want to ask, why did I put the drawings in? The short answer is "for fun!". My magazine articles have got quite a lot of serious stuff in them, so I thought that a little light relief would help and would break up the text.

Anyway, thank you for reading so far, and I hope that you will enjoy some of the other parts of the book and perhaps find help and inspiration here and there. I am very happy to dedicate this book to the clergy and people of the parish of Solihull, to those of you who have read some of my articles already and made kind comments, and to many other parishioners who have been supportive of me and my family, especially during difficult times.

To God be the glory!
Martin Tunnicliffe

---

[1]  *I also include some articles that I contributed to the publication "Mike's Musings" before it ceased publication. It was a newsletter for the congregation of the Solihull St Michael's District Church.*

# PART ONE

# *Medley*

# Common Prayer: Common Worship

Solihull Parish Magazine September/October 2012

Talk to a member of the Prayer Book Society and I guess that you will soon be informed that this year [2012] marks the 350th anniversary of *The Book of Common Prayer*. The book (sometimes called the *1662 book* or simply the *BCP*) appeared at a time when our country was struggling to find its equilibrium after the upheaval of civil war. It was a time when religion and politics were as enmeshed here in Britain as they are in the countries of the Middle East today.

Fortunately for the Church of England, and for those many worshippers who today still value and use the *BCP*, the book did not need the combined authority of Church and State to ensure its survival. It has stood the test of time because of its intrinsic excellence as a practical liturgical text and book of devotion for both clergy and lay people. It does have deficiencies and limitations, but in spite of these, the *1662 book* remains a document of great worth, based on centuries of sincere Christian devotion expressed in a style of English that is both elegant and beautiful.

And the book is memorable!

When I was 8 years old, I learnt by heart a number of Prayer Book Collects. I should point out that this was not because of childhood sanctity. It was because, at that time, I spent a long holiday with a particularly devout Aunt. Not only did she attend church regularly: she also conducted morning prayers in her living room. What endeared her to me more than this was the fact that she used to give tuppence (2d) as a reward to any child who learnt the Sunday Collect off by heart. Consequently, my repertoire of learnt Collects tends to cluster around the later Sundays after Trinity, because that is when the holiday occurred.

For all that, I have never ceased to be thankful to my Aunt, for I value those BCP Collects, together with all the other bits of the 1662 Prayer Book that, through constant use, are lodged in my memory. They have become a valuable spiritual resource. In the account of his time as a hostage (*"Taken on Trust"*), Terry Waite tells us that he was deprived of books at the start of his ordeal. During that bleak period, he records how he was sustained and upheld by the Book of Common Prayer. He was able to call to mind large portions of the Prayer Book which he knew by heart because of early Christian nurturing and habitual worship.

## Variety or confusion

The *Book of Common Prayer* (often in the carefully revised 1928 text) formed the standard liturgical diet for the Church until the 1960s when the new forms of worship began to be trialled. Some people may lament the demise of the older forms, but we should not allow sentiment and nostalgia to colour our judgment. Liturgy is too important for that because it is the people's common prayer and worship. Churchgoers, even occasional or irregular ones, are well aware that during the past 50 years there has been a veritable explosion in liturgical reform. To those who, like me, were brought up on a "take-it-or-leave-it" style of worship, the new services and variety of presentations may sometimes seem like confusion and muddle. But the need for change and development in the Church's patterns and styles of worship has been deeply felt for over 150 years. The Church's new prayer book, Common Worship launched in 2000, had to happen, and we need to accept it and work along with it, even if we may not take to it at first.

Very wisely, our modern prayer book reformers kept the 1662 Prayer Book as an authorised liturgy for the Church of England. This decision was taken not just to please the old guard or preserve the beautiful language even though it may do both these things. We keep the *BCP* because it provides the Church with a sound basis for our worship and prayer. This is because it is founded on those basic principles which under-gird the whole of our Christian faith: loving God, and loving your neighbour as yourself: principles set in the Old Testament books of Deuteronomy (6.5) and Leviticus (19.18) and clearly endorsed by Jesus in the Gospels (Matthew 22.37-39; Mark 12.29-31; Luke 10.27). This summary of the Law of Moses is usually considered as being two-fold: love of God and Neighbour. Actually, it is three-fold: love of *God*, of *Neighbour*, and of *Self*. There is an interesting psychological truth expressed here. For if you do not love your Self as a treasured child of God, then you cannot in all sincerity love either God or your neighbour. I want to take these three principles in turn and make a brief comment on each:

**Love of God**  This is best shown in *God-centred* prayer and worship. There is a tendency in the revised liturgies contained within the new books to move away from this ideal of God-centredness. Common Worship seems to provide endless choices for individual ministers to pick and choose from. Under these circumstances, it is easy for the spotlight to turn away from God and his heavenly glory, and towards the individual minister or other worship leader. The danger of that is rather well described by Evan Daniel in a textbook on the *Book of Common Prayer* written for students over 100 years ago. The style may be a bit flowery, but the point is effectively made when he writes:

*The practical advantages of having a Book of Common Prayer are sufficient in themselves to recommend and justify its use. A moment's thought will show that fixed forms of prayer are an indispensable condition of common prayer; for how can we join with one accord in offering up our supplications before God, unless we know beforehand what we are going to ask?*

*What an advantage too it is for a congregation, in offering up their prayers, not to be dependent on the memory, or fluency, or idiosyncrasies, or health, or varying moods, of the minister who conducts the service. However devout and able he may be, he may neglect to mention many things that ought never to be omitted in common prayer; he may give an undue prominence to matters in which he himself takes a special interest, or to matters of transient importance that already occupy too large a share of the congregation's thoughts; he may repeat himself to the point of weariness; he may divorce prayer from those cardinal doctrines of religion upon which prayer should always be made to rest, and from which all its hopes are derived; he may foist into his prayers matters that do not belong to prayer at all, and that ought to appear, if anywhere, in a sermon; he may hesitate, and falter, and grow confused, and so distract his hearers in the midst of their devotions. On the other hand, where a fixed form of prayer is used, as in the Church of England, the congregation are quite independent of the minister in offering up their prayers. They are always sure of being able to pour out their souls to God in carefully digested forms of prayer, the product of ages of piety, such as no individual mind, however gifted and cultivated, could hope to rival on the spur of the moment....How vastly superior, then, (are fixed forms of common prayer) to any extemporaneous effusions.*

**Love of self** This does not mean self-indulgence; it really means having a balanced attitude towards oneself which implies self-knowledge, self-criticism, and self-sacrifice. This is accepting oneself as a child of God, made in his image and a product of his love. A sound common liturgy connects with this personal aspect of the Christian life, because the familiar patterns of public worship resonate in one's private prayers. In my younger days, along with many of my contemporaries, I was given a Book of Common Prayer by a godparent. We carried it to church on Sundays, but we also kept it by the bed at home. So there was a meeting point between *Common* prayer (i.e. community prayer), and *private*, or personal, devotion. Evan Daniel again:

*[The Book of Common Prayer] is a manual of* public *prayer, and, considered from that point of view, its order, its variety, its fixed language, are helps, not hindrances. In our closets, and by our family hearths, we may, if we like, pour forth our hearts freely in the language which our hearts suggest; but even there our devotions will often be assisted by the use of pre-composed forms. Our mind will be kept from wandering by the words before us, and our* real *needs will not be lost sight of in the urgency of the need of the moment. Besides, we can always read 'between the lines' of our Prayer-book, and make those petitions* particular *which are expressed in* general *terms.*

*It is an exaggeration to say that our Prayer-book does not meet particular exigencies; for not only are all its prayers large in expression, and wisely comprehensive in structure, but in the Litany, the Collects, and 'Prayers upon Several Occasions,' will be found special petitions suitable for almost every conceivable occasion calling for common prayer. Surely it is not necessary, in addressing (God) "who knoweth our necessities before we ask," to specify on every slight occasion our needs by name.* Common *prayer does not exclude simultaneous* individual *prayer; and every thoughtful worshipper will mentally refer the general petitions of the Liturgy to particular needs, whether public or private, which are uppermost in his mind.*

**Love of neighbour** Our Book of Common Prayer is God-centred; and in private devotion, if we are truly honest with ourselves in our self-appraisal, the formal prayer of the *1662 Book* will be helpful as we relate to God *personally*. It is only a short step from these two considerations, love of God and of Self, to love of Neighbour. The closer we are in our relationship to God in worship and prayer, the more real and urgent will be our Christ-like concern for others, for their health, well-being, and salvation. The *BCP* is not just a Sunday book. It is an everyday book, and it can be used to great effect in intercession, at home as well as in church. Increasingly these days, as I watch, read, or listen to the news, words from the BCP come to mind: "Lord have mercy upon us … we have offended against thy holy laws … forgive us our trespasses." So praying, we enter into a kind of spiritual solidarity, not only with the sufferers, but also with the perpetrators of sinful acts who "have erred, and strayed from thy ways like lost sheep." "Save us, and help us, we humbly beseech thee O Lord." The world is desperately in need of our common prayer.

The Book of Common Prayer was launched in 1662 by an Act of Parliament known as the Act of Uniformity. As a kind of 'one-size-fits-all' exercise, the book was supposed to unify the nation. It manifestly failed to do so. As an unintended consequence, in the turmoil that followed the

Act, a considerable boost was given to Non-Conformity, which in the long term was no bad thing for the Church of England. The lesson to be learnt is that, in matters of Christian liturgy, however excellent any particular Prayer Book may be, "one-size-fits-all" is not a workable system. Reform of the liturgy just has to happen from time to time in order to meet the changing needs and aspirations of succeeding generations. People who appreciate, value and revere the old texts must not simply dismiss with scorn the endeavours of the modern reformers.

Having said that, the Church of England does well in keeping the 350-year-old book, or a good deal of it, as a living and workable text for worship and prayer, so that our Church continues to see the need for dignity, formality, and beautiful language in the conduct of common worship. We can indeed be thankful for our Book of Common Prayer, for its compilers, and for all those who have loved and valued and used it during the past 350 years. Its continued use, even if sparse, will inspire those who use it and future worshippers in their Christian pilgrimage.

⸺⟨○⟩⸺

# Do Dogs Have Souls?
### Solihull Parish Magazine October 2007

… or as the question is sometimes put, "Will my pet go to heaven?" Years ago we had a family dog called Sal. She arrived as a black ball of mischievous fluff, ate voraciously, and grew almost visibly until she became a rollicking and badly behaved adolescent. Her uncertain parentage endowed her with a shaggy black coat which seemed to sprout in all directions. Her long legs often appeared to want to go towards various points of the compass at the same time, and the word "obey" was most definitely lacking from her vocabulary.

One of Sal's ancestors must have been a retriever. As a puppy she retrieved everything. Unmentionable articles of clothing from anyone's room, sticks, stones, fire-irons, mushrooms, long-dead worms, clothes-pegs, even spent matches, were dutifully and continually laid at your feet in the hope that you would pick them up (ugh!) and throw them. She once excelled herself by retrieving the mixing bowl in which my mother had left the bread dough to rise in the heat of the sun outside the kitchen door. Naturally, Sal had first devoured the contents, and the yeast working inside her had the same effect as several large whiskeys. She staggered round the house and garden in a bemused state of intoxication, bumping into things and behaving not unlike our village drunk returning home on a Saturday night.

## Visiting

As children we were not all that fond of Sal, for we had not really recovered from the loss of our beloved Doodles, the small, nondescript and slightly neurotic terrier-like mongrel that we had been brought up with. So we generally gave a sigh of relief when my father (who was a country vicar) went visiting his parishioners and took Sal with him. If our feelings were somewhat cool towards the dog, our verger's attitude was definitely hostile. We never learnt how relationships had broken down between them. I suppose Sal had retrieved his verger's gown or a few altar candles and been the victim of some vigorous reprisal. But she never went near the church, and always skulked off to her basket whenever Bert called at the vicarage.

With old Mr Farley, though, things were different. He was Sal's best friend. For one thing, he lived at a respectable distance from the village across several rabbity fields. So visiting Mr Farley provided a good opportunity for exercise and sport, and at the end of the walk, while my father and Mr Farley kept each other occupied with parish gossip, past and present, Sal was regaled with scrumptious biscuits and bones on the fireside mat.

In due time, old Farley fell sick. The distress my father felt as he ministered to him during what became his last illness was not shared by Sal. The more frequent visits meant more walks, and of course more tit-bits, because Farley's fondness for the dog never diminished. In fact, their relationship seemed to grow deeper. Having deposited a piece of well-chewed twig (or perhaps some less salubrious object) by the bed, Sal appeared to sense that it would no longer be hurled good-naturedly out of the cottage door for further retrieving. So she made no further demands, and instead she would sit quietly by the bed, allowing Farley to tickle her ears with a hand which was becoming more and more like the sticks he used to throw for her.

## The Funeral

The village turned out in force for the old man's funeral. We all stood in respectful silence as my father preceded the coffin-bearers down the aisle of our little church, now rather uncomfortably full of unaccustomed worshippers. Farley's coffin was placed reverentially on the bier at the front of the church, and the bearers decorously withdrew as my father prepared to begin the service.

At that moment there was a slight agitation among the congregation, and heads began to turn like corn stalks in a mild summer breeze. I peered round the edge of our family pew back down the aisle and saw, to my complete astonishment, our dog Sal, trotting sedately towards the front of the church which, like many a disgruntled parishioner, she had assuredly never entered since her altercation with the verger. She carried, as usual, something in her mouth which was too small to be identifiable but which looked to me suspiciously like a desiccated worm she had just retrieved from the churchyard.

Sal arrived at the coffin, eyes twinkling and tail erect, its black plumes of unkempt hair waving gently as if in mourning. The congregation was motionless for a moment. Then I saw the verger, with a gleam of malevolence in his eyes, make a slight movement towards the dog. My father gave him a withering glance and he seemed visibly to shrink back into his prayer-desk. Sal, apparently aware of the mute consent of my father, sat down quietly beside Farley's coffin, holding the small, blackened worm in her mouth rather like a diminutive cheroot.

There she stayed, unmoving, for the whole service. And at the end, she solemnly followed the bearers as they carried the mortal remains of old Farley to their last resting place. There, at the graveside, Sal stood with the mourners, her black plumes waving in the cool wind. "Earth to earth," said my father, "ashes to ashes, dust to dust." The undertaker sprinkled some earth on to the coffin, and Sal, clearly sensing the conclusion of the matter, dropped her worm beside Farley's grave. Then, with a dignity quite unlike her normal boisterous self, she quietly turned and walked away without so much as a side-long glance to any of the throng of potential stick-throwers.

Do dogs have souls?

I wonder!

# Exclusive or Inclusive?

Solihull Parish Magazine June/July 2005

*"I am the way, the truth, and the life; no one comes to the Father except through me."*

John 14.6

There can be few sayings in the Bible that have been so grievously distorted, misunderstood, and hurtfully and mischievously misquoted as this one. For generations, there have been un-thinking and ill-informed Christians who have blindly assumed that this text proves beyond all doubt that only baptised or born-again Christians are allowed into God's kingdom of love, and that anyone else is excluded. If this were true, then that would mean that there is no place in God's home for anyone who lived before the first century of the Christian era. And there would be no place for anyone who, since then, has belonged to any other religion. This, of course, is blatant nonsense. And fortunately there have always been Christians, probably most Christians most of the time, who have felt uncomfortable about this exclusive stance.

In this connection, it is wonderful to see, in our own lifetime, the growing awareness and mutual understanding that there has been across the religious and cultural boundaries. This has led to a tremendous rapprochement between the various Christian churches, as well as between Christians and those of other faiths. All of this, of course, can do nothing but good. I would contend that the devil does not like this trend one little bit, and will do everything in his power to prevent it: hence the upsurge of violent nastiness in our world today. It is the backlash of one who knows that he is facing defeat. It must be acknowledged, however, that this text from John 14 remains to tease and puzzle us, and I am afraid that it is still a kind of battle cry for Christian fundamentalists, who will insist on trying to take the words of the Bible literally rather than to engage with them intelligently. Can we, then, approach this text in a positive and constructive way? The answer is, yes, we most certainly can, provided that we can see it in the wider context of the whole Bible, and particularly of the gospel.

It is well known that John's gospel is quite different from the other three, and is written in such a way that it carries many layers of meaning. This means that it takes a great deal of time and meditative thought as well as intellectual effort to unravel its secrets. Go to any theological library, and you will find whole shelves of books about John's gospel which bear witness to that fact. In an article as brief as this, I just want to highlight two important points, or pointers, for consideration.

## Creative Interaction

The first takes us directly into the *mystical* dimension in the Bible, and a little way into the prayer life of Jesus. It is quite clear from the New Testament that Jesus had a phenomenally deep and close mystical relationship with God, whom he referred to most frequently as "Father". We know how special and loving this relationship was, because Jesus often used the familiar and informal word "Abba" in his prayers, which is the Aramaic word equivalent to our "Dad" or "Daddy". I am not aware that any other Jewish rabbi, or, indeed, any other religious leader of any tradition that I have come across, ever expressed such intimacy in their relationship with God. It was certainly a religious custom, long before Jesus, to consider God as Father. But the living and creative interaction that Jesus had with the Father was obviously very special, if not unique. And this became the mainspring of all his thoughts and words and actions.

This relationship was so special, so close, and so loving, that when John came to write about it in his gospel, some 50-60 years after the death of Jesus, he found himself driven to express it as a *one-ness*, a mystical unity … "I and the Father are one … he who has seen me has seen the Father" (John 10.30 & 38; 14.9-11; 17.21). And with enormous daring, John has Jesus saying from time to time "I AM." Now, "I AM" is the very sacred and mystical name of the supreme God. It was held by Jews to be so sacred that only the high priest was allowed to utter it. This "I AM" was the name and nature of the hidden God which was first revealed to Moses at the Burning Bush (Exodus 3.14). But in John's gospel, it becomes attached to Jesus: "I AM the bread of life … the light of the world … the good shepherd" (John 6.35; 9.5; 10.11 et al).

Here it is again in our text: "I AM the way, the truth, and the life. No one comes to the Father except through ME" … that is to say, except through the I AM. In other words, anyone who truly seeks and finds, in prayer, this mystical, mysterious, yet loving and creative relationship with God, the I AM, is actually in fellowship with Jesus, whether they realise and acknowledge it or not. Notice also that, remarkably, in this saying, no conditions are laid down, no labels or qualifications are required. No one comes to the Father except through I AM. Or, to put it positively, *anyone* who explores that living, prayerful relationship with God, is doing so through I AM, and is therefore in mystical relationship with Jesus. No wonder the church has always rejoiced to say and to sing about Jesus, in the words of the Te Deum, "Thou hast opened the kingdom of heaven to *all* believers".

## Mystery of suffering

This leads to the second point, or pointer, in understanding this text. If you use a reference Bible, you might find a link between this verse (John 14.6) and a saying of Jesus in Matthew 7.14: "Enter through the narrow gate ... the gate is narrow and the way is hard that leads to life". The link word is "way" (sometimes translated as "road"). "I AM the *way* ... the *way* is hard ...".

One of the key aspects of the Christian gospel message is that Jesus invites his followers to join him "along the way". This is a glorious road, joyful and fulfilling. But it is also, and unavoidably, the way that leads to, and through, pain and suffering and crucifixion. The implication is clear. The gospel gives us the opportunity, in a manner that is, I think, quite unique, to make some sense of suffering, and even to see its creative potential in the overall Divine plan. Once again, this blessing is not reserved to Christians, but is open to anyone. There are many non-Christians who, in fact, accept the way of the cross, often with a greater understanding and courage than many Christians.

I once came across a living example of this when I visited a bereaved family. They were not "religious" in any conventional sense, and church connections were very tenuous. But there was something about the demeanour of the woman, recently widowed, and of her sister who was helping her, and of their elderly mother who lived with them – some spiritual richness that I found hard to define but which was quite palpable. I discovered in the course of conversation that the husband who had died had been diabetic, also that he had had a leg amputated, and that he had had a heart condition, and in addition, as a result of the diabetes, he was blind. It was altogether a grievous affliction over a six-year period. But in all this, he had been totally uncomplaining, and continually grateful for the attention and care that he had received. He had also clearly had a rich and creatively loving relationship, not only with his wife, but also with his elderly mother-in-law. Here was evident the reality of suffering and pain, yet at the same time a glimpse of the glory of that hidden relationship between the human and the Divine – the Flesh and the Word.

"I AM the way, the truth and the life. Anyone who comes to the Father is coming through ME" (i.e. through the I AM). If we are to begin to grasp the meaning of this Saying, then it is essential that we do not just read it and assume that we know what it means; we need to reflect on it and ponder over it in the wider context of God-relatedness, which is meditation leading to prayer. Such meditation and prayer are part of our spiritual pilgrimage. As such, it is not reserved to Christians, but is open to anyone – ultimately to all human beings. Yet Christians have a special part to play in it. We tread the road joyfully with Jesus and with one another. We accept with Jesus the narrow limitations imposed by suffering and pain, in sure hope of the glory of our common destination and, in His name, we invite others to do the same.

I know that texts such as John 14.6 are indeed puzzling and leave many unanswered, and sometimes unanswerable questions. As I grapple with them, I often find myself turning to the 19th century hymn by F.W. Faber of which the first line is "There's a wideness in God's mercy" (or in some hymn books, "Souls of men why do ye scatter"). They make an apt conclusion to the thoughts expressed in this article:

*There is grace enough for thousands*
*Of new worlds as great as this:*
*There is room for fresh creations*
*In that upper home of bliss.*

*But we make his love too narrow*
*By false limits of our own:*
*And we magnify his strictness*
*With a zeal he will not own.*

*For the love of God is broader*
*Than the measures of man's mind;*
*And the heart of the eternal*
*Is most wonderfully kind.*

## *St Ninian's Chapel, Whithorn, Scotland*

Part of my 70th birthday gift from the family was a holiday in Scotland, and Irene and I stayed in Newton Stewart in Galloway. Not far away was the little seaside port of Whithorn. I was attracted to it because of its connection with Saint Ninian, known in history as The Apostle to the Picts. That's about it, really, because there is no reliable evidence about him beyond tradition and legend.

My personal connection is that I was baptised (September 1931) in the church of Saint Ninian in Whitby, so I feel that he shares with my patron saint some of the heavenly oversight due to me within the communion of saints. So I felt drawn to draw Saint Ninian's Chapel. The church dedicated to him in Whitby was very "high" and my baptism service was wreathed in clouds of incense, so I'm told. In recent years it got so "high" that it splintered off from the Church of England and became an independent congregation. I'm not sure, but I think it became Roman Catholic and than splintered again so that it could continue to celebrate High Mass in its traditional, but no longer permitted, ritualistic manner. I tried to look it up on the Internet, but the site was blocked, so perhaps it's even too "high" for cyberspace.

# Firm foundations for ministry

*... a fragment from the author's hidden life*

Mike's Musings 2006

I suppose, now that it's on the Internet, it must be public knowledge, so you might as well know the story.

I studied for my degree at The University College of North Staffordshire (now known as Keele University). During the past year (2005) the University's alumni officer has launched an Internet chat-line where former students can share information and reminiscences. This has been well patronised by those of us who were among Keele's first-ever students. We were guinea-pig undergraduates during the 1950s at Britain's first post-war, and experimental, university.

One chat message recently mentioned the name of a firm which immediately rang bells with me, at the same time inducing a slight flush of embarrassment: "Silhouette". How often had I seen that name while ascending and descending on London's Underground escalators, the letters flanked by a scantily dressed young lady in undergarments! It goes without saying that I always turned my gaze ... (she was, of course, as frequently posted on the opposite wall).

Well ... all good things come to an end, and the final year at Keele inevitably came round, with its dread warning, not only of impending exams, but also of finding a way of earning one's living in the big wide world out there. Was it, perhaps, the fact that I was disheartened by the failure of a few job applications which prompted me to respond to a notice on the board in the Students' Union announcing that "Silhouette" was looking for a graduate trainee for their sales department?

Be that as it may, I was called to interview in London and met with the friendly and smartly-dressed sales director at his Mayfair office. He took me out to lunch. It was at a Lyons Corner House, and I recall that it was not very good. I dare say he appraised my student attire and found an eating-house appropriate to my rather impoverished appearance. Anyway, we had a friendly chat, about this and that, carefully avoiding for the most part any reference to female undergarments. After lunch we parted on friendly terms with mutual recognition that I was probably not temperamentally suited to sell ladies' underwear. Thank goodness he paid my rail fare. And also thank goodness that I had retired from active C of E ministry before this became public information!

I ended up with Messrs. Gestetner Ltd, if you want to know, servicing and selling duplicating machines: from softwear to hardware, you might say.

# God Speed
### Mike's Musings May 2006 (revised)

Kosuke Koyama was born in Tokyo in 1929. After taking his first degree in Japan he studied further in the USA, gaining his doctorate from Princeton Theological Seminary in 1959. From 1961 to 1969 he was a missionary in Thailand, teaching in a seminary there. From Thailand he moved in 1969 to become dean of the South East Asia Graduate School of Theology in Singapore. In 1974 he left to teach religious studies at the University of Otago in New Zealand. After 1979 he taught at the Union Theological Seminary in New York. Koyama is best known for his *Waterbuffalo Theology* (1974).

In 1979 Koyama published *Three Mile an Hour God*, a further collection of biblical studies related to South East Asia. In the chapter from which the book takes its title, he contrasts the instant efficiency of modern technology with God's way of teaching his people. God took forty years to train them in the wilderness – at walking pace (3 m.p.h.). In the classroom we learn theory, but God teaches us through real-life experience. 'Forty years in the wilderness' points to God's basic educational philosophy. The rest of the Old Testament bears this out.

"God walks slowly because he is love. If he is not love he would have gone much faster. Love has its speed. It is an inner speed. It is a spiritual speed. It is a different kind of speed from the technological speed to which we are accustomed . . . It goes on in the depth of our life, whether we notice or not, whether we are currently hit by storm or not, at three miles an hour. It is the speed we walk and therefore it is the speed the love of God walks."

I immediately thought of this when, some years ago, I saw a video clip of Bede Griffiths in India. He was a Roman Catholic Benedictine monk who dedicated his life and spirituality to bridging the divide between Christianity and Hinduism. He was born England in 1906 and educated at Christ's Hospital in London and Oxford University. He died in India in 1993. Without ever relinquishing his Christian faith and priesthood, he lived as a Swami on his own ashram in India.

In the video clip, the camera is following him as he sits contentedly facing backwards, his legs dangling, on a cart drawn by a bullock. With a smile he says, "I am now travelling at the average speed of the rush-hour traffic in New York." He might have said London, or Birmingham, or almost any other modern city. Bede Griffiths certainly knew about God-speed, and his books are well worth reading.

————————◦————————

# Heaven and Hell

*(The two articles which follow go together as a single unit. They were published in successive months because of space)*

## Heaven's Above? I don't think so.
Solihull Parish Magazine April 2017

I begin with a question that I cannot answer. How many people today believe in 'heaven up there', with God, Jesus, Saint Peter, and some (perhaps not all) of our deceased relatives and friends looking 'down' on us? Whether or not the question can be answered, I am sure that, like me, you will have listened to eulogies at funerals where the speaker finishes by looking upwards as they recall some particular memory, perhaps even addressing the dead person as if they were within hearing distance some-where above the church or chapel roof.

Now a rhetorical question: is it not today impossibly naive to hold on to the notions of heaven and hell as regions located above and below the earth, and is it not high time that the Church got rid of them? In the light of our understanding of the universe, we must surely move on, and find new ways of expressing traditional teachings of this kind, or simply be held to ridicule.

So the big question now looms: what are we going to put in their place? To this, I can only offer a personal view for your consideration. Let me begin with two quite solid facts that need to be borne in mind. In the first place, no one has ever been to heaven and then returned to tell us all about it from their personal knowledge. So all accounts of heaven (and there must be hundreds if not thousands of them) must derive either from creative imagination or from a kind of knowledge which is different from the usual factual kind. Secondly, in spite of this, discourse about heaven has always been taken seriously by religion. In Christianity, neither the Bible nor the Church treat heaven as a kind of fantasy, even though there is a tendency to use extravagant and poetic/symbolic language when heaven is being talked or written about.

The last book in the Bible, the Revelation to John, immediately comes to mind. But set that aside for a moment, and you will find that, on the whole, the New Testament is more earthly than heavenly. Christianity is an incarnational religion in which the physical/material stuff of our everyday world really does matter. In his teaching, Jesus appears to avoid speculation about heaven as a region or entity in itself. Instead, he places a good deal of emphasis on what he called "the kingdom of heaven (or of God)". My key text is the statement that Jesus made to the scribe in Mark's gospel (12.34), "You are not far from the kingdom of God." I reckon that those words are spoken to us as much as to a first century Jewish scholar.

## Spiritual domain

For myself, I am happy to abandon any notion of a geographical or spatial heaven. I believe in heaven as a spiritual dimension, a mode of being which I experience as existing always close by and alongside the world that I know. Visions of thrones and crowns, angels and archangels, white-robed throngs and incessant noise (however musical) – this is not for me, even though they appear in the Bible. But a nearby spiritual dimension or domain in which God's will is done and to which we may have access in this mortal life as well as in the life-to-come, that is as real to me as the physical world which is provided for me as a small part of my total existence.

How do I know about this nearby heaven? I made mention of a kind of knowledge that is different from our usual kind of knowing about things. This is the spiritual perception which has always been part of what it means to be human. A friend of mine recently published a book on spirituality which he entitled "A sense of more than".[2] I can't think of a better way of expressing in simple terms the human faculty of spiritual understanding which even 300 years of scientific enterprise, technological advance, and materialistic philosophy have not been able to suppress or explain away.

This capacity for spiritual understanding and experience gives us glimpses of heaven: feelings of total joy and satisfaction beginning with the experience of love and loving, and then including those times of supreme contentment when we are uplifted by the beauty of nature or of artistic expression. Those of us who choose to nurture our spiritual faculty in religious observance will sometimes, perhaps often, be given more glimpses of the heavenly dimension. These will lead us to respond in prayer, praise and worship. And there are times when some of us have been so overwhelmed by an experience of heaven that it is impossible to find words to describe it. This perhaps is more common than you may think, and can happen to people outside as well as inside any specifically religious context.

One final thought. We say in the Lord's Prayer, "Thy will be done on earth as it is in heaven". For me, these words emphasise the closeness of, not the distance between, heaven and earth. There is no doubt that God's will *is* done on earth, for if it were not, the world would cease to exist. If we like, we can choose to freewheel through life unthinkingly, vaguely hoping that God's benevolence will favour our day-to-day existence and keep us as free as possible from too many setbacks. But if we pray the Lord's Prayer, then we are challenged to keep an eye on the spiritual dimension and actively live in such a way that heaven and the goodness of God remain firmly on our agenda.

In this article I have given, as I said, a very personal (and rather sketchy) view of heaven. Perhaps it is more of a discussion document. So if you do open up a discussion, please count me in!

—◇—

---

[2]  *'A sense of more than'* by Tony Michael Martin. Published in New Zealand by Makaro Press.

# Fire down below? I don't think so
## Solihull Parish Magazine May 2017

It seems only logical to follow up an article on Heaven with one about Hell. Once again we are dealing with a concept with a long train behind it of religious tradition, teaching, and imaginative speculation. I have been helped in formulating what I have to say by H.A. Kelly's book *Satan: A Biography* (C.U.P. 2006).

Having just read my thoughts about Heaven, you will not be surprised when I say that I completely reject any notion of Hell as a place of hot torment, ruled over by the Devil and populated by a mixture of demons and nasty human beings whose sinful lives on earth have ended. That whole scenario should be consigned to the rubbish bins of history and the fertile minds of stand-up comics. It is not biblical and was very largely created by the medieval Church, partly to reinforce its desire to control faith and morals, and partly as a kind of psychological safety-valve for the human imagination, rather like the horror films of a later generation.

Having said that, the idea of a Devil and a place of posthumous punishment does occur in the Bible, but not in the lurid detail in which the medieval Church loved to portray it. On the occasions that the Bible refers to the subject, it just seems to be trying to cope with the perennial and intractable problem which besets us all, namely, the puzzling existence of sin and evil. Simple justice demands that if wicked people don't suffer in this life, then there must be a 'place' in the next life where they will get their come-uppance. Unfortunately there is no evidence to support this view. The Bible passages that one can point to are sketchy, confusing and contradictory.

The hoofed and horned Devil of popular imagination has no place in the Bible. In the Hebrew Old Testament (e.g. in Job) you will find reference to a mythical figure called "a satan", which means an accuser, tester or adversary. And this still seems to be the sense in the New Testament, as in the story of the Temptations (testing) of Jesus. When the Greek version of the Hebrew Scriptures appeared in Alexandria 200-300 years before Christ, the translators used the word "diabolos" for a satan, from which we get our "devil". Sometimes they added the definite article "ho" (the). This gives the impression of personalising "diabolos" which in turn inadvertently opens the way for future centuries to elaborate the personification of evil virtually at whim.

## Complex

The history of ideas about Hell and the Devil is as fascinating as it is complex. Kelly's book has over 300 pages, and he refers to an academic study on the subject published in the 1980s which runs to four volumes! Setting that aside, for practical purposes we are still left with the everyday problems of evil and human nastiness which are ever-present realities within the context of the sovereignty of the loving-wise-powerful God who is above all and through all and in all.

I have happily jettisoned the Devil and Hell, but certainly not the reality of evil. One thing that needs to be stressed is the falsity of those who claim to be in touch with evil powers. They may describe themselves as Satanists or black witches. Such deluded people may well be able to display strange powers, but this simply derives from their misuse of the psychic element in human nature. It has nothing whatever to do with the "principalities and powers ... the spiritual forces of evil in the heavenly places" mentioned by St. Paul in Ephesians 6.12.

In my previous article I expressed my belief in the spiritual dimension in which the kingdom of God may be experienced both here and here-after more intensely than is common during our earthly life. I would now add my belief that this dimension is by no means free from the malignity of evil. However, when we are considering the life of the spirit, it is no good looking for information and guidance to the misguided people who meddle in psychism, often with malicious intent and for their own manipulative advantage. If you want to learn about the reality of evil and the spiritual strategies for dealing with it, you must go to the saints of God. And of course you must go in the company of Jesus who is our, and the world's, supreme guide and mentor during our pilgrimage towards God.

As with my previous article, I recognise that this one is likely to raise more questions than it answers.

**Great Malvern Priory**

It is not often that you can find a spot where you can sit and sketch a large and imposing church from above. So this was an unusual pleasure, with my back to one of the Malvern Hills. The town and its lovely setting has been a favourite place to visit for longer than I care to remember. The number of drawings in my sketchbook made within a radius of two or three miles of this church bears witness to that.

One day I was sketching a panoramic view from the Southern end of the hills near the British Camp. My young companion at the time had a dodgy hold on English history. When we passed the sign to the British Camp and were walking up the incline, he said, "Where are the lorries?" It was hardly the sort of track that an HGV driver would choose, and I was puzzled for a moment. Then I burst out laughing (which I really shouldn't have done) when I realised that he assumed we were approaching an army camp! Sadly, I wasn't given the opportunity to draw a Bronze Age army lorry.

The Priory was founded by a religious order during the 11$^{th}$ century and building began soon afterwards. It was greatly enlarged in succeeding centuries and carefully restored by Gilbert Scott during the 19th century. It reputedly displays the largest collection in England of 15th -century stained glass.

———◦———

# "Hi"
### Solihull Parish Magazine September 2017

I am trying to reconcile myself with the fact that I might as well join the new millennium. So I am beginning some of my email messages with the greeting "Hi" instead of the traditional English formula "Dear xxxx…" Fortunately I don't currently have a correspondent called "Jack." I admit to being slow to adapt, because I reckoned that "Hi" was just another unfortunate habit that we had picked up from North America, like OK and Father's Day. However, a little reflection tells me that there is more to the greeting "Hi" than the mere apparent laziness of using two letters and one syllable to greet people.

"Hi" is clearly short for *Hallo* (or *hello* if you prefer), a greeting which actually reaches way back into ancient history. When I went on pilgrimage to the Holy Land, I was intrigued by the Arab children calling out what sounded like *hallo* as they tried to sell us their postcards and sticky sweets. I discovered that they were in fact saying *shalom* (or *salaam*) the common Middle Eastern greeting which was already ancient when Jesus and his disciples used it. In effect, *shalom* (Arabic *salaam*) and *hallo* share the same etymology as well as the same depth of meaning. The greeting is normally used casually, and the standard translation from Hebrew is "Peace", but the concept is much broader.

Our greeting has a common root in an ancient Indo-European word *qoilos* meaning *healthy, intact, well-omened*. This became *holos* in Greek *(whole, complete)* emerging in the English *whole, wholesome, hale (and hearty), hail*: and, significantly for us, *holy*, (or *hallowed*). So when you say *hallo* to someone, you are wishing them not only peace, but also health and wholeness, well-being, prosperity and holiness. If you can do all that in just two letters, well – why not!

## Holiness

In religion, the word "holy" has added value. It has to do with something special. We think of the separate-ness of God. And holy people and holy places are manifestly, and yet mysteriously, apart from the normal run of everyday life and, in one way or another, closer to the Divine. From the scriptural Christian standpoint, we may recognise that Jesus was

born into a nation that was expert in holiness. Individually and collectively they may sometimes have made an unholy mess of things (who doesn't, sometimes), but in fact the Jewish tradition was admired among many foreigners for its holy writings, its holy priesthood and its holy temple, all of which ideally supported and promoted exceptionally high moral and ethical standards. In spite of this, when the prophecies about the Messiah

were fulfilled, and God became so shockingly close that people could touch and be touched by him, the tradition could not accept it.

The trouble was that Jesus redefined the whole idea of holiness. He mixed with 'unholy' people and had them among his entourage. He challenged the regular holy people with his teaching and often got the better of them. He even challenged the Holy Temple itself, the visible centre of holiness, and foretold its destruction. He touched the untouchables and thought the unthinkable. Finally he turned a completely unholy death into a focus of holiness for all subsequent generations.

His followers, both the ones he knew personally and the others who came later, were sometimes drawn from among people whom the strict Jewish tradition would consider unholy. But they considered themselves to be part of a new idea of holiness. The idea was based on the tradition, and Peter, in his first letter, accepts the moral and ethical standards of the Old Testament and quotes the Word of God from the book Leviticus: "It is written, *you shall be holy, for I am holy.*" But then he goes on to tell the new followers of Jesus: "*You* are a chosen race, you are a royal priesthood, you are a holy nation, you are God's own people."

So holiness is no longer a matter for experts, for professional priests, and for stone temples. It is something which belongs to ordinary people. I wish there was more space to explore the link between health and holiness. We have already seen the linguistic connection, but there has to be a very practical link as well, because you cannot have true health without holiness. Suppose our NHS became a National Holiness Service. Now there's a thought to end with!

# Missing the mark
## Solihull Parish Magazine January 2013

I think it was the U.S. President, Calvin Coolidge, who was reputedly short on easy conversation. When he returned home from church one Sunday morning, his wife asked him if he had enjoyed the service.

"Yep."

"And was it a good sermon, dear?"

"Yep."

"So, what was the sermon about, dear?"

"Sin."

Seeking a more satisfactory response, Mrs Coolidge said: "Yes, dear. But what did the preacher say about sin?"

"He was agin it!"

At a time when we are beset with problems relating to violence and crime of an intensity that is little short of alarming, perhaps the time has come to give this unfashionable topic more prominence, both in private reflection and in public discourse. When there is an upsurge in violence, crime or scandal, people naturally start looking for causes. And they come up with a boringly repetitive recital, ranging from "it's the parents", via "it's the schools", and ending up with "it's the government". In our present culture, whenever something unpleasant happens, whether a suicide bomb, a street riot, or simply tripping over a paving stone, we tend immediately to look for someone to blame, and, if possible, to shame, perhaps with a lively hope of gaining some financial compensation.

I would venture to suggest that we are in danger of missing the point altogether. We are ignoring a very basic and very human cause of trouble, summed up in the three-letter word S-I-N.

The fact that the word has fallen out of fashion is as much the fault of the Church as it is of anyone else. During the past 100 years or so, we have allowed psychiatrists and comedians to take over much of the discourse about sin. Psychiatrists have taught us how to explain it away, and comedians have shown us how to trivialize it. So I think the Church, i.e. every Christian person, has a massive task to keep sin on the agenda of society. That means we need constantly and consistently to re-educate ourselves, and, as far as possible, other people about sin. If we fail to do this (and I believe that we are failing), then we shall be colluding with sin, and we will ultimately have no one to blame but ourselves for the fraud and violence which are the natural consequence of sin.

The Bible could be thought of as a kind of specialist textbook on sin. The Old Testament is full of it, and from the New Testament we take the key Christian teaching that Christ died for our sins. When we bring to mind the word "sin", our imaginations will produce all kinds of lurid pictures, so it is very important to look at the definition. When we come to study the actual Bible text, it is surprising to discover that the word mostly used in the scriptures that we translate by our word "sin" actually means "missing the mark". In the ancient world, this word was used of a sling-stone that missed the target, or an arrow that went wide.

**Making the point**

Many years ago I used a dramatic visual aid to illustrate my sermon about sin. We set up a full-size archery target in the church at the front of the central aisle at the chancel steps. I then recruited a local member of the Woodmen of Arden to give me a brief archery lesson. She shot first from the back of the church, and successfully embedded an arrow in the Gold. Then it was my turn. I think the congregation were holding their breath. But I shot from halfway down the aisle, not from the back. Happily, my arrow also got the Gold. I should have said that we tactfully moved the choir from their stalls behind the target before the experiment! I think that the point was effectively made. If either of us had "missed the mark", then someone may have got hurt. Sin is missing the mark, shooting wide of the standards that God, in his love, has set up for us. And because of it people get hurt, and sometimes very badly hurt indeed. How, then, do you deal with it? It seems to be endemic in the human race. It is as well to ask how it is dealt with in the Bible.

In the Old Testament there are all kinds of elaborate procedures for dealing with sin. In the ancient world, sin and crime were much more intermingled than they are today. So you find judicial punishment dealt out for both crime and sin. And, of course, you also find very complicated procedures connected with sacrifice and priestcraft and temple worship. But there are two factors of key significance in the Bible in coping with the problems of sin and evil:

- The Bible teaches that all ethical and moral standards derive from God. The focus for all goodness and right behaviour is Divine, and sin is indeed a missing of the mark, shooting wide, a deviation from the Divine intention.

- The other relevant biblical theme is the all-pervading possibility and reality of forgiveness. Forgiveness, whether from God or from other human beings, is always factored in as a counter-balance to sin. Without forgiveness, all human existence would be doomed to failure.

It is very obvious today that both these things, God's standards and the need for forgiveness, are widely ignored in our society. This lack of understanding needs to be taken much more seriously both by the Church and by the nation's leaders. In the first place, in their blindness and ignorance, people are attempting to replace God's standards with moral and ethical standards of their own, based on expediency and often with no better guide than the volatile media and the all-pervading Internet. Secondly, the spirit of forgiveness far too often gives way to calls for revenge, punishment, and compensation.

**Act now**

This all appears to be very portentous and serious, and it may seem to be beyond our reach to do much about it. That is by no means the case. If Christians don't do much about it, then I doubt very much if anyone else will. Being practical, I would suggest three definite and positive courses of action:

- We need to be more honest with ourselves as weak and fallible human beings. We should keep doing a quick personal audit of our thoughts and feelings and actions to see where we are really going wrong. And when we do fall short of God's standards, let's not be so ready to make excuses for ourselves. If we have sinned, then we have sinned, and that's the long and short of it.
- We have prayers of General Confession in our prayer books. We should use them more often than just on Sundays. I still prefer the words in the Book of Common Prayer: "We have erred and strayed from thy ways like lost sheep: we have followed too much the devices and desires of our own hearts." This is not just a personal prayer. The pronoun is "we", not "I". There are times when I don't personally feel any great sense of sinfulness, but I find the General

Confession seriously meaningful when, for example, I hear or see or read about some of the horrific items in the news. And then I pray more fervently: "Yes, Father, we *have* erred and strayed from thy ways … we humans have offended against thy holy laws …" And the prayer then becomes an intercession for the perpetrators of fraud, violence, and other crimes against humanity, as well as for their victims. "Have mercy upon us, miserable sinners."

• We can reflect more deeply on the words in the Lord's Prayer, "Forgive us our trespasses, as we forgive those who trespass against us". Forgiveness is a transaction that can happen and does happen between us human beings, and also between God and the human race. If that were not the case, then humans would have destroyed each other long ago, and been obliterated from the earth. By our own attitude, we can either enhance forgiveness, or we can slow it down. So, "Forgive us our sins, as we forgive those who sin against us". Thinking about those words should help us to identify any personal grudge that we may be harbouring, and to ask for God's help to deal with it.

Those are three practical points for personal consideration and prayer. Perhaps the time has come for a new call for national repentance. If you look at the opening chapter of our oldest Gospel, St Mark's, you will find both John the Baptist and Jesus doing just that, in clear imitation of their predecessors, the Old Testament prophets. When things got really tough in national affairs, far from looking for someone to blame, they called the people to repent and confess their sins.

One final point. Sin is deviating from God's standards, missing the mark, shooting wide, resulting in hurt for other people as well as a lowering of self-esteem on our part. In archery, the nearer you are to the target, the more likely you are to hit it. Our Christian target is Jesus Christ himself. The nearer we are to him, in prayer and action, the more likely we are to get things right.

# Psychic Fairs
## Solihull Parish Magazine May 2014

Look up "Psychic" on the Internet and you will find a welter of occultism. Among other key words in this connection are Astrology, Aura, Animal Healer, Clairvoyant, Crystal, Divination, Dowsing, Magic, Medium, Palm Reading, Pendulum, Spiritualism, Tarot, Wicca, Witchcraft. Vocabulary borrowed from the authentic religious tradition includes Church, Healing, Meditation, Spirit, Spiritual, Soul.

If you have not already done so, sooner or later you are likely to come across a Psychic Fair in your area. In some local pub or hall there will be a gathering of people connected with what we may call the psychic "trade". It is a trade because the psychic and the occult are big business and vulnerable people can readily be relieved of their cash as they pursue the apparent opportunities open to them to acquire arcane knowledge or power, or to get healing, peace of mind, or success in love or money-making. The question is, what should be the Christian response to all this, whether individual or local church?

There are two extreme reactions that are NOT helpful. One is to rubbish the whole psychic rigmarole as utter nonsense and pour scorn on those misguided people who get mixed up in it. The other is to label it as the work of the devil and to mount some kind of crusade against it under a Christian banner. Both these attitudes are counter-productive.

**Psychism**

In the first instance, psychism is not nonsense. The psychic is an undeniable factor of our being animal and human. There are certainly plenty of charlatans connected with the psychic "trade" just as there are rogue traders in other walks of life. But they exist because of an authentic ingredient in the natural make-up of human beings. This is the mysterious and largely unknown psychic component that lies in the depths of our sub-conscious and un-conscious areas. The psychic realm is a real part of each human being and, collectively, of the human race as a whole. The so-called sixth sense, which we all experience at some time in our lives, is a manifestation of this. It is the tip of a large iceberg, most of which is out of sight, if not exactly out of mind.

It is equally unhelpful to brand all psychic happenings as anti-Christian and therefore diabolic. Psychism is a natural endowment deriving from humankind's evolutionary past, rather like fear, laughter, using our imagination, and the pleasures of sexuality. As such it is morally neutral. As with other natural gifts, psychism can be developed and used for either good or ill, or it can be ignored altogether and left to atrophy.

One obviously good use of psychic gifts is for healing. Alongside the conventional and scientific study of medicine, it is generally agreed that people do have natural healing gifts. Such gifts vary from person to person and from time to time. Another positive use of our psychic capacity is in the development of our spiritual, religious and godly capabilities, for the psychic and the spiritual interact, as do the physical and the spiritual.

## Shadow side

On the negative side, just as ploughshares can be turned into swords, so psychic gifts can be developed for unsavoury purposes by people of ill-will, for financial gain or self-aggrandisement, or in order to influence, dominate, control and therefore harm other people by means of magic, sorcery, witchcraft and satanism. The question of evil spirits runs alongside occultism and psychism, touching at many points. But this is a separate issue, having a theological dimension that the psychic and occult areas do not (or only to a far lesser extent).

## Christian response

What then is the Christian stance to be? The biblical basis is clearly set out in the texts whose references are at the end of this article. Briefly, the received wisdom is that people should have as little as possible to do with occultism in any of the forms encountered in Psychic Fairs or anywhere else. This is not because it is necessarily dangerous or immoral in itself, but simply because in Christ (that is, in the revelation of God in Jesus Christ through the Holy Spirit) occultism of any kind is not necessary. It is not spiritual and has nothing to do with authentic spirituality. Psychism as a natural human endowment may be subject to scientific study and research. If Christians have any particular psychic gifts, such as healing or second sight, they should dedicate them in prayer to God in order that they might be rightly directed or, alternatively, be taken away.

Living in a scientific and so-called enlightened age has not diminished people's fascination with matters connected with the occult and "supernatural" phenomena. Rather curiously, interest in this area has increased greatly in recent years. One reason is the decline in institutional religion. When there is a lack of spiritual interest and understanding, dabbling in the psychic will often fill the vacuum for some misguided people. Much of this will be both neutral and harmless, but the potential for exploitation, danger and damage is always there, especially among the weak and vulnerable. Christians and the Church need to remain vigilant.

If there should be a Psychic Fair in the neighbourhood, it is unwise for Christians or the Church to mount a campaign against it, because that will only give it gratuitous publicity and therefore be counter-productive. It may be a sensible move for church members to be warned not to have anything to do with it, and clergy should offer prayer and spiritual counselling to anyone caught up in occultism or troubled by it. Every Church of England diocese now has a team of accredited advisers who are available to help in this domain if necessary. It is certainly unwise for church premises to be let out to groups such as psychic fairs, and the old-fashioned idea of having a "Gypsy Rose Lee" to read palms at a Church fete is definitely out. Check out these references from the Bible:

| | | | | | | |
|---|---|---|---|---|---|---|
| Leviticus | 19.31 | 20.6 | 20.27 | Deuteronomy | 18.9-14 | |
| 1 Samuel | 28.3-25 | | | 2 Kings | 21.6 | 23.24 |
| Isaiah | 8.19 | 19.3 | 47.9 | Jeremiah | 27.9 | |
| Malachi | 3.5 | | | | | |

| | |
|---|---|
| Acts | 16. 16-18 |
| Ephesians | 5.11 |

***Leigh, Worcestershire***

As the owner of this property came towards me while I was drawing his house, I felt a slight *frisson* of dismay. However, he proved to be friendly, made a not uncomplimentary remark about the half-finished sketch, and reliably informed me that "Leigh" is correctly pronounced "Lye". I wanted to ask what sort of rooms the oast houses made inside but he left before I got the chance.

Two other nearby features have attracted me to visit this lovely spot several times. Out of sight behind the oast houses is an enormous 14th century tithe barn which, in the Middle Ages belonged to the monks of Pershore Abbey who owned much of the land in this part of the county at that time. English Heritage care for it, and they inform us that it is the largest cruck barn in Britain, with roof beams made out of single oak trees. It is well worth visiting, and, what is more, you can get in for nothing!

Then, just off to the right of my picture, over that wall, is the medieval parish church of St Edburga. It's one of those churches which, for me, has a palpable 'atmosphere'. (You might think that every church ought to have this, but it varies, and many do not for some reason that I cannot fathom.) So I love to spend time there in solitary silence. What is more, they have a rather nice piano, which I have enjoyed playing sometimes, but please don't tell anyone.

# Swords and ploughshares
### Solihull Parish Magazine October 2010

These are two implements that don't much figure in the lives and experience of most of us, but you might hear them mentioned in Church if you attend a Remembrance Day Service in November. They are referred to by the prophet Micah in the Old Testament, and he may well have had first-hand, or at least second-hand experience of both. In this chapter he is using the words figuratively to describe the process of peacemaking: "They shall beat their swords into ploughshares" (Micah 4.3). Our thoughts on Remembrance Sunday need to be along these lines.

The traditional Remembrance Service is quite straightforward. We continue to long for, and to pray for peace, and rightly honour those who have died in battle or as a result of warfare. It is good, too, that we should have public acknowledgement of the ongoing work of our armed forces; that we should applaud their courage and skill, and remind ourselves of the dangers to which they may be exposed. It is right to retain this annual opportunity to focus our attention on human conflict and the need for adequate defence for the realm against aggression. At the same time, we call to mind the continuing need for peacekeeping operations which are intended to protect vulnerable and innocent people who may be victims of violence or terrorism.

So we remember the war dead, among them perhaps even close relatives or friends, or those who recently have suffered violence or outrage. Now is also the time to raise questions about some of the deeper issues of our time, as the world situation appears to become more problematic by the minute. The beating of swords into ploughshares means the harnessing of human energy, expertise and technology for peaceful purposes. This is certainly a prophecy that can be fulfilled. To some extent it has been fulfilled and we are all the better for it. The "sword" of nuclear fission, which was thrust so tragically into the heart of Japan in 1945, has become a "ploughshare" of nuclear energy. Although far from being problem-free, this resource means that countless numbers of people benefit from relatively inexpensive electricity, and for sixty-five years the world has managed to avoid the calamity of another atomic bomb.

If you read Micah's words carefully, you will notice that he sets the fulfilment of his prophecy not in the present, but in what he calls "the last days". That means, at some point in God's future. This is because the prophet is at pains to remind us that there is an ever-present temptation lodged in the human heart to turn ploughshares back into swords, and this lies not far beneath the veneer of what we think of as civilisation. The writer Lawrence Durrell has a character in one of his novels who puts it like this: "Two thousand years of civilisation! It peels off like a flash. Scratch with your little finger and you reach the woad or the ritual war paint under the varnish! Just like that!"

We may well be currently successful in controlling and inhibiting nuclear arms, but the manufacture of weapons of piecemeal destruction is still very much alive, whether these be Kalashnikovs or cluster bombs. The plough-share of peaceful and fruitful trading is constantly being turned into the sword of the arms trade. It seems likely that the high standard of living that we have come to enjoy in Western society is partly the result of that nefarious market. The recent and ongoing economic crisis is surely due to the ploughshare of fair trade, honest dealing, sharing of profits, and concern for others being turned into the sword of sharp practice, dishon-esty, greed and acquisitiveness. We may rightly point the finger at the rich and powerful, but it is an easy matter for any of us to transform our own ploughshares of generosity and decency into swords of self-protection and consumerist greed. So the prophet's words are there to remind us all to be constantly vigilant in our own attitudes, behaviour and self-restraint, lest we collude with the negative powers of destruction, and leave the world a worse, instead of a better, place for our having passed through it.

## More than just remembering

Remembrance Sunday is much more than remembering the dead. The modern world is a confusing place; even war is no longer simple because, in the traditional sense, we no longer have obvious enemies, or if we do, we don't really know who they are. The confusion is largely due to the pace of change, which is why it is good to use Remembrance Sunday as an opportunity to reflect about some of those vital things that never change but which we are in danger of neglecting. I recall the inimitable Rabbi Lionel Blue speaking on BBC Radio 4's *Thought for the Day* about some of these. He quoted Isaiah: "Buy bread without price". Then he said: "I thank God each day for everything I get for nothing … the economic crunch points us towards a simpler life."

That strikes me as being a vital lesson to be learnt by the peoples of the developed countries of the world. We have jacked up our expectations far too high. We expect to have a vast number of choices in our supermarkets, to eat more food than is good for us, to have instant solutions to our health problems, to live to a ripe old age free from pain, and some people appear to expect not to have to die. To thank God each day for the good things of life that cost nothing is an excellent corrective. As Lionel Blue put it, "The best things have no price: a kiss, a compliment, some encouragement, forgiveness, a joke, feeling needed, the glow that follows a good deed: these things are priceless." So as we remember the dead, let us also remember and give thanks for the good things of life.

———◇———

# The miracle of feeding
Solihull Parish Magazine May 2010

The story of Jesus feeding five thousand people with just five loaves and two fish is told in the sixth chapter of Saint John's Gospel. It is sufficiently familiar not to need re-telling (if necessary you can refresh your memory by looking it up). Bible scholars down the centuries have poured out their learning and their ink producing commentaries on the Gospel of Saint John. I am hoping to provide a simple and direct comment on one sheet of paper that will give not a learned discourse, but a lively challenge for the reader, because I believe this is what the story intends.

In our global village, the hungry multitudes have become uncomfortably close. We have been reminded of this, regularly and stridently, during the past sixty years. During that time, the problem of world hunger has not only persisted, it has got worse. The gap between rich and poor has widened, both nationally and internationally. This fact should sit naggingly on the consciences of Christians, and of any right-thinking and good-living person who enjoys more affluent living standards. One clear message comes through from the story of the feeding of the five thousand. By God's grace, and in accordance with his promises, there _**is**_ sufficient "for everyone to have a little". God has, God does, and God will provide. _We_ may think in terms of shortages. The Bible thinks in terms of promises.

You may have noticed, for the Gospel writer has made it plain, that this story is an echo of the story of the miraculous provision of manna which is told in the Old Testament book of Exodus, chapter sixteen. There, through the intercession of Moses, God provides the hungry with bread from heaven. In the Gospels, Jesus is sometimes considered as a new Moses. So the same miracle happens again: bread appears, apparently from nowhere, and the hungry are filled, if not "with good things", at least with a sufficiency of daily bread for the time being.

## Hungry at home

There are, however, subtle differences in the tale as it is told by Saint John. As I was thinking about those differences, I found my mind wandering back many years. I remembered my mother performing miracles of feeding during the nineteen-forties. I am sure that she wasn't the only mother to have done so at that time. During the early years of wartime rationing, my parents had five dependent children at home between the ages of nought and sixteen. Three of us were teenage boys, and we had appetites! I sometimes look at the cheese that I put in a couple of sandwiches these days and think: _that was about a week's cheese ration for one person in 1942._ It is then that I begin to understand that my mother must have been a worker of miracles. I also realise that the miracle of mothering was more subtle than just putting food on the table. The children's hunger was satisfied partly because the parents were willing to go without. In addition, and most importantly, the satisfying of emotional and spiritual hunger was also high on the family agenda. My mother taught us all music, and myself and my sister to play the piano. She saw to it that we attended church, said our prayers, and were properly disciplined and respectful in the home.

This wartime domestic scene is, I suppose, fairly unexceptional. But there are connections with some of the subtleties embedded in the story of the feeding miracle in John's Gospel. One fairly obvious example is the sacrifice of the lad who was willing to give up his picnic. John seems to be suggesting that this act of simple generosity was crucial to the whole operation. In our present society, a principal cause of family breakdown is parents who are putting their own happiness and well-being before that of their children. In the wider scenario, a principal cause of world poverty is the heavy reluctance on the part of the better off to lower their high standard of living. The word "sacrifice" is not prominent in our vocabulary. The boy and his picnic are a quietly persistent challenge to us all.

## Hors d'oeuvre

In the Gospel story, the crowd's need for food was obvious, and Jesus was able to meet it in some mysterious way by God's grace; however, that crowd had not actually come to be fed. John says that they were attracted by Jesus' healing power. Jesus himself was more concerned about the deep spiritual hunger in the whole nation. "Man does not live by bread alone." Those words from the book Deuteronomy in the Old Testament were clearly in the forefront of the Lord's mind on this occasion as they had been when he fasted in the wilderness.

If you read the rest of chapter six in John's Gospel, you will soon understand that the feeding of the crowd is a mere *hors-d'oeuvre* to the main course. The Jewish nation in the time of Jesus was embedded in tradition and embroiled in unsavoury politics. It was in danger of becoming spiritually bankrupt, as our nation is today. They needed desperately to hear the Word of God afresh. Jesus was called and commissioned to proclaim it, as the Church is called and commissioned today. So the climax of this story is not the full bellies of the crowd, it is Jesus proclaiming, "I am the bread of life … I am the true manna which comes down from heaven … Man does not live by bread alone, but by every Word that proceeds from the mouth of God."

In the miracle of our family wartime feeding, we have already seen that it wasn't just a matter of doling out food to hungry mouths. The owners of those mouths had a role to play as well. We were schooled in the virtues of orderliness and fair play. We learnt from each other as well as from our parents that "man does not live by bread alone". Fair shares, values of honesty, generosity, decency and good order were as much part of the nourishment as food.

It is interesting that in the Gospel story of the miraculous feeding, Jesus says, "Make the people sit down". An undisciplined crowd on their feet can be a menace, as we know from modern hooliganism. In fact, in Mark's Gospel, it is reported that the crowd is not only seated, but grouped into orderly lots of fifty and a hundred, an interesting detail.

In the current global problem of aid for the poorer nations, we know that the provision of resources is vital. We also know that it is, on the whole, futile to pour in money and food unless there is some responsibility shown at the receiving end. The beneficiaries must learn that they need to exercise discipline and order. They must also counteract fraud and corruption, and make valid attempts at self-help. Otherwise a culture of dependency is created and the poor are, in the longer term, no better off. The same applies in the handling of our domestic policies. I think the matter can be simply stated. On the part of those who are better off, more emphasis could be placed on the need for sacrifice. On the part of those who are less well off, more emphasis could be placed on the need for discipline and order. When that happens, then a little can go a long way, just as it did in our days of food rationing: and miracles can happen.

—◀◦▶—

# The Prodigal Son: new light on an old story
*[This article was published in two parts in successive months.]*

## The Prodigal Son Part One
Solihull Parish Magazine May 2013

The wonderful parable of the Prodigal Son in the fifteenth chapter of St Luke's Gospel ranks among the world's greatest and most-loved stories. Backed up by Rembrandt's heart-warming masterpiece of the returning son being embraced by his father, the story is usually taken to be a vivid illustration of how the overwhelming love of God reaches out to welcome home the penitent sinner. Thus have innumerable sermons and commentaries presented it, and quite correctly. But is that all there is to it? By no means! Behind the disarmingly simple façade there is a depth of meaning and wisdom which commentators and preachers seldom tap into.

To begin with, we should take into account that New Testament teaching, including that of Jesus, is set against a background of thought and ideas which are radically different from ours. In our modern Western civilization we tend to think that we are somehow placed in, and are part of, a comprehensible universe in which all things are subject to scientific laws, and what we don't now know about it is simply waiting to be discovered in due course. Also, most of what is real and significant and important to us as individuals is held to be contained totally within the span of earthly life that is allotted to us, within the boundaries of birth and death. That is not the thought-form of most of the human race before the 18th century, and generally is not that of non-Western cultures today. Broadly speaking, ancient and traditional wisdom considers that the most important feature in the universe is the spiritual dimension against which all human life dramas are played out.

In this scenario, the Prodigal Son, who leaves home with his share of the inheritance, falls into a disreputable lifestyle, comes to his senses and then returns home to a loving parent, stands for every human self working out his destiny[3]. He also represents the whole human race collectively playing its part in the drama of salvation. The story is in three parts that mirror the three main stages of human development: childhood, adolescence and maturity. In traditional wisdom, our created existence as persons (selves) is not constrained within the limits of birth and death. Each of us individually, and all human beings corporately, are held in eternity within the loving purposes of the all-loving, all-wise and all-mighty God who is the Supreme Self. Wordsworth expresses it well in his famous Ode on the Intimations of Immortality:

> *Our birth is but a sleep and a forgetting:*
> *The Soul that rises with us, our life's Star,*
> *Hath had elsewhere its setting,*
> *And cometh from afar:*
> *Not in entire forgetfulness,*
> *And not in utter nakedness,*
> *But trailing clouds of glory do we come*
> *From God, who is our home.*

---

[3]   The Prodigal Son is of course male, but stands for every human being. In this article I am using the masculine form simply because it becomes tedious and clumsy constantly to use the 'his/her' format. I invite you to make your own adjustment as you read.

At our conception we are given a physical body in which to work out our destiny in accordance with a scheme that God in his loving wisdom has ordained, yet which paradoxically includes our free will.

Our birth and childhood, then, constitute an essential separation from the Divine Self, the womb of the Spirit, in order that we may begin the process of growth in spiritual consciousness that can in due time lead us back to the spiritual home where we truly belong. In the parable this is evident when the father, without demur, allows the son to go off with his inheritance to the "far country". is His riotous living there is not sin. The son wastes his substance without any qualms because he is still in the state equivalent to the irresponsible innocence of childhood. He is in spiritual babyhood, enjoying the merely conscious life of the physical body. At this stage he is virtually asleep to his true Self.

**Adolescence**
The second stage is adolescence, for the human self must needs grow and develop. Dissatisfied with childhood, the teenager pushes the boundaries as he seeks independence and freedom. Paradoxically, the more freedom he aspires to, the more his life is characterized by insecurity, conflict, and the burden of responsibility. He tends to reject the traditional values he was taught, but the values with which he replaces them are unreal. The parable describes this period as being "in want" at a time of famine. The adolescent turns to his peers in preference to his childhood mentors, but their situation is no better and they can do him no good. So he has to live in a pigsty and starve, deprived of the benefits of time-honoured spiritual values based on the divine attributes of truth, beauty and goodness.

This dire situation, however, is actually the kick-start for spiritual growth and development. However painful, confusing and chaotic it may be, this stage cannot be avoided. What applies in the case of the individual is also true of human societies, and we shall look at this aspect in the second part of this essay next month.

At precisely this low point of hellish existence, the story moves to part three with the telling phrase "he came to himself" (his-Self). The suffering adolescent suddenly has a glimpse of his true Self, which of course is a counterpart or "image" of the Supreme Self (Genesis 1.26 reminds us that we are created in God's image).

This is the crucial turning point in the process of salvation. The son recognises the worthlessness of his own self in this situation of "want". In sharp contrast, he recalls the abundant love of the father and has a glimpse of the (spiritual) riches that he had forfeited back home. "How many of my father's servants have more than enough while I am starving here." So begins the return journey. And if the "country" to which the son travelled is "far", the journey home must be equally so. In the Bible (Old Testament) this return journey is told in terms of the spiritual pilgrimage through life undertaken by God's people as they journey from the bondage of Egypt (the far country) towards the Promised Land (the Father's home). It is a struggle, with a constant temptation to relax and slide back ("they wished themselves back in Egypt" Acts 7.39 referring to Numbers 3.4-5). But the all-powerful love of the Father ineluctably draws the Prodigal Son homeward into union with Himself (His Divine Self), for this alone is perfect freedom.

This is the destiny chosen for the Prodigal Son (ourselves) "before all worlds". It constitutes the purpose of our creation. At birth, and in a sense during childhood, we are in a dreamless sleep. We begin spiritually to reawaken in adolescence. This waking process is accompanied by nightmarish dreams, the pigsties, starvation and servitude in the parable. But in the divine order of things, they blessedly goad us towards the full awakening into maturity. If we have any doubts about the supremacy and depth of God's love, Jesus adroitly dispels them, for he tells us how, even before we have completed the journey, and while we are still "afar off", the Father comes running to meet and embrace us and welcome us "home". And then comes the party to celebrate! All the suffering and agony of having been in the far country is now seen as the negative pole in the full creative process of which the positive pole is joy.

I can already hear the question, "What about the elder son?" (Luke 15, verses 25-32). You must wait for the second part of the essay next month before we find the answer to that.

◇

# The Prodigal Son Part Two

I believe that we do Jesus less than justice if we read this parable as a story made up simply to tell us about God's love for the penitent sinner. This interpretation is superficial and does not take into account the rich and inspiring background of traditional thought uncluttered by modern scientism and materialism. The story in Luke 15 relates to the ultimate purposes of God, the Supreme Self, who is not only all-powerful (almighty), but all-wise and all-loving in his creative purposes for humankind.

I mentioned in Part One how each human being, created as an individual "self" by and within the love of God, the Supreme Self, is given this life to fulfil his or her destiny. Our lifespan on this earth, individually or collectively, is but a mere fragment of our total existence, which abides within the context of eternity. Consequently, God's plan for us must completely transcend our earthly existence in ways that we cannot at present comprehend. Nevertheless, traditional teachings as well as our own experience show us that our spiritual (God-ward) growth towards Self-consciousness (which is God-consciousness) has broadly three phases. As previously mentioned, these are analogous to birth and childhood (the phase of innocence), adolescence (the phase of awakening), and maturity (fulfilment in the Father's love). The parable clearly follows this pattern in outline, so now we need to ask ourselves two questions, *who is the Prodigal Son*, and *who is his older brother?*

The conventional answer would be that the Prodigal Son is any sinner who repents, but I have already said enough to indicate that this does not go far enough. When we read the first chapter of Genesis, we usually think of Adam as representing the whole human race, together with Eve of course (in Hebrew, the word "adam" means "man"). In the same way it makes good sense to consider the Prodigal Son as representative of all humanity, for we are all, each one of us, "children of God". We are "selves", who are endless differentiations of God, who is the Supreme Self. The parable can be seen as the total story of humanity. As such, the three stages that I have identified merge together as part of the whole drama of God's continuous creative process. In other words, the parable is happening here and now, and encompasses the whole experience of the human race.

## Periphery

In spiritual terms, God *is*. There has never been a time when God is not. And God is One. But God is also Love; consequently he manifests himself (his Self) by breaking this unity into diversity, and by creating endless "selves" in his image who can learn to respond to his love. It is God's loving purpose that he gives human beings the freedom of separation from their Divine Source so that they may learn freely how to make their response. So in the parable, the father makes no demur when the Prodigal Son leaves home, regardless of the risk and the suffering that must ensue. For God in his wisdom knows that this is the only way in which true love can operate. God is the spiritual Centre of all that is, and his loved children must in due course find themselves at the periphery of the circle of existence, living, moving and being in the physical universe, which in the story is "the far country".

This is the location and environment which we call "the world". Here in the world, as in the story of Adam and Eve, we must "fall" before we can grow spiritually and find our way back to the Father, for however dire and painful the consequences of our separation from "home" must be, the Father never ceases in his longing to draw us back to himself. The actual life story of Jesus himself is embedded in the parable. The sending of Jesus the Christ into the world "for us and for our salvation" seems very like the letting go of the younger son in the story. So Jesus himself is, in a sense, the Prodigal Son who "learns obedience by suffering" and is "tested as we are", subjected to the same process involving the pain and suffering that separation from God inevitably brings about. Reference is made to this in the Epistle to the Hebrews (5.15 & 5.8).

The story of the Prodigal Son actually makes sense of the world as it is. The human race is, as it were, in the second stage of the story, the adolescent phase of spiritual awakening. This is where society experiences the swings and oscillations of the growing youth. From being merely conscious in the sleepy innocence of childhood (the garden of Eden), the youth begins to awaken to self-consciousness, but he mistakenly puts his fallen self into the centre. He co-operates with his fellows, but does so for his own ends and interests. So his fallen self becomes a travesty of his True Self. Real values become hopelessly distorted: freedom becomes licence, wisdom becomes cunning, strength becomes violence. All this is our experience in human affairs on a local, national or global scale.

Fortunately the story does not, indeed cannot, end there. Such states of affairs cannot be endured indefinitely, and every age has its witnesses to the goodness, beauty and truth of God the Supreme Self who continually calls us "home", drawing us ultimately to that inexpressible consummation of unity in Himself. So the end is an outburst of rejoicing, party clothes, dancing shoes, and a great feast. Our homecoming merits a party, joy in heaven, laughter in Paradise. Do we not see the same thing happening when Zacchaeus and Levi each throw a party after Jesus helped them severally to "come to themselves"?

So we finally come to consider the elder son and his complaining. This appendix seems designed to emphasise the reality and security of our spiritual destiny as belonging within the loving embrace of God in spite of everything that can go wrong along the way. The main thrust of the parable is completed by the rejoicing. So my surmise is that the elder son represents the angels. Created as pure spirits, they are (in the words of the parable) "always with me (i.e. the Father), and everything I have is yours". The implication is that God's human creation, including Jesus, having endured the suffering and "overcome the world", are in a sense superior even to the angels who are never subjected to the same process. The same idea is hinted at in Psalm 8 and expounded in the first two chapters of Hebrews.

I am suggesting that the parable of the Prodigal Son has a far greater depth of meaning than is usually given to it by commentators and preachers. As such, it requires a correspondingly greater depth of reflection and meditation on our part. To enable this, I would urge you to look up the biblical references I have given, and the ones below, and ponder over them. You may come to see how they tally with the message of the parable as I have tried to interpret it.

Jeremiah 1.5      Hosea 11. 1-2       John 13.34; 16.33  Ephesians 5.14
Romans 8.21      Hebrews 10.5; 12.2

*[Note. In my exposition of the parable of the Prodigal Son, I have drawn freely from chapter 4 of "The Threefold Reality" by R.G. Coulson (published privately 1966). The book is out of print. If you would like to borrow a copy please visit www.contemplative-prayer.org.]*

**St Peter and St Paul South Petherton**

I was staying in a Somerset retreat house near this town. I went for a walk one sunny afternoon, and couldn't resist this octagonal tower. One or two passers-by made encouraging remarks while I was drawing it so I thought I'd include it.

What I didn't know at the time is that South Petherton is just a mile away from the Fosse Way. Running about 200 miles from Exeter to Lincoln, this Roman road is one of the longest in England. "Fosse" means "ditch", and it is surmised that along the route, there might have been a kind of defensive ditch, of which nothing remains. Some of the major roads that we use today are built on top of the Fosse Way.

Another church very close to the Fosse Way is dear to my heart. This is St Gregory's in the Warwickshire village of Offchurch near Leamington Spa. "Offa's Church". This is the place from where King Offa ruled his kingdom of Mercia during the 8<sup>th</sup> century. He was the builder of that other spectacular "fosse" known as Offa's Dyke. It was intended to keep the Welsh out, or in, depending on your point of view. Either way it never worked, much to the advantage of both Wales and England. It didn't occur to me that two of my retreat venues, in Warwickshire and in Somerset, were linked by a Roman road. Come to think of it, it would have been much easier for me to draw a Roman road: all that is required is a ruler!

# The Psalms: a personal view
Solihull Parish Magazine July 2015

I have to admit that when I began to study theology I was not best friends with the Psalms. They seemed to me to be obscure, irrelevant, and ungrammatical. In church they were well-nigh impossible to sing: hymns were much more fun! As a student of English, some of the poetry appealed to me: who could fail to be moved by Psalm 23, the song of the boy-shepherd! Or the poignant lament of the exiles "by the waters of Babylon" (Psalm 137). However, my teachers (and the books I read) constantly told me how those 150 songs of Sion were a veritable treasure-store of prayer, praise and spiritual enlightenment. I now know that to be true, but it took many years and a good deal of spiritual discipline to find some of the keys to that treasure-store and to appreciate the treasure.

One key was "Repetition". The Psalms were selected and assembled together after the Jewish people returned from the Babylonian exile: that was about 400-500 years before the time of Jesus. They became an official hymn book for the Temple in Jerusalem, as well as a prime resource for worship and prayer in synagogues and Jewish homes. Practically every Jew would have known most of the Psalms by heart. They were a kind of spiritual wallpaper. In the first century, the Christian Church based its patterns of worship on the Jewish tradition, including the singing and recitation of the Psalms. After 2000 years, that tradition still persists. When I was at theological college, I entered more deeply into this tradition as we recited

Morning and Evening Prayer in chapel every day. Down the ages, monasteries and other religious houses have used the Psalms as the keystone of their offering of worship. When I was ordained, I accepted the discipline of reciting a Daily Office of which the reading of the Psalms was the backbone.

In itself, this discipline did not provide an instant understanding of the Psalter, but it did give me some more keys, which, over the years, have opened up this spiritual treasury. For instance, I sometimes found that the Psalmist was praying with me as a kind of fellow pilgrim. If I was feeling very down-in-the-dumps, I could be reading "my soul is full of trouble … thou hast laid me in a place of darkness, and in the deep" (Psalm 88), or "Save me O God, for the waters are come in even unto my soul; take me out of the mire that I sink not" (Psalm 69). Alternatively, if life was good and I was feeling joyful, I could find myself reciting "Praise the Lord O my soul, and all that is within me praise his holy name"(Psalm 103).

**Surprise**

Naturally, there are also times when the words of the Psalm don't tie in with one's own personal feelings. This led me to discover another important key. Although many of the Psalms are deeply personal, almost egocentric, they represent a *community* at prayer. So if the words that I am reading or reciting don't apply necessarily to me at the time, they certainly apply to someone else. So, for example, I may be reading from Psalm 55 "The ungodly cometh on so fast for they are minded to do me some mischief, so maliciously are they set against me." At the time of reading, I am not under threat myself, but there are others whom I know, or that I have heard about in the news, who most certainly are. So the words of the Psalm immediately become my prayer for them.

Occasionally I am taken by surprise by a simple phrase. Not long ago, during Morning Prayer, I read the opening words of Psalm 33 "Rejoice in the Lord O ye righteous, for it becometh well the just to be thankful." I suddenly found myself thinking of one or two of the people I know who are good, kind, and upright citizens but who are not Christian. The words instantly became a prayer for them to recognise the love of God in Jesus Christ. On another occasion, I was brought up short when I read in Psalm 89 "I have made a covenant with my chosen." I recalled how the relationship between God and Israel, and between Christ and the Church, is likened in the Bible to a marriage bond. So those words have become a prayer whenever there might be a time of strain in the home.

This leads to another important factor in the use of the Psalms in Christian prayer and worship. I used to wonder why I should have so often to be trawling through Jewish history. The answer is that, under the new dispensation inaugurated by Jesus, we are now able to see the symbolism that lies behind these ancient biblical texts. Thus, whenever we come across the words "Sion", "Jerusalem", "Israel", "Judah", we are at liberty to substitute the word "Church", for the Church is the new community of God's people. Try it! In the same vein, when reference is made in the Psalms to King David, Abraham, Moses, or Jacob, it is quite legitimate to be thinking of (King) Jesus, his disciples and other Christian saints and leaders "throughout all ages".

Continuing this symbolic theme, the words "Egypt", "land of Ham", and "field of Zoan" represent any oppressive regime or culture in any generation including our own (as does Babylon in the book Revelation). And while we are thinking of what we might call "the geography of salvation", let us remember that "the promised land" is no longer simply a narrow strip of territory on the East side of the Mediterranean Sea. Our New Testament clearly teaches us to broaden our horizons, for "God so loved *the world*." The holy (or promised) land is indeed this planet, the earthly home (albeit temporary) for all God's children. If you had any doubts about the Psalms (or indeed a good deal of the Old Testament) being relevant to us today, they can be dispelled, especially in these days of globalisation and concern for the planet.

## Smiley Postscript

My mother, who was very devout, nevertheless always maintained that God must have a sense of humour because "he created the elephant." She knew the Psalms in the 1662 Book of Common Prayer version very well. As she approached middle age and her figure became more rotund, I heard her mutter with an air of resignation, quoting from Psalm 139, "Ah well, '*thou hast fashioned me behind and before*'"!

# The Sermon
## Solihull Parish Magazine 2015

Ours is an era of slick visual presentation fuelled by the increasingly sophisticated modern technology of television, computers and social media. So the sight of a clergyman in a pulpit, standing six feet above contradiction, talking to a congregation sitting in attentive silence seems unbelievably out of date, if not dinosauric. For many people, the very words "sermon" and "preaching" have a nasty flavour, and suspicions arise of being treated like a child. Probably most of you who read this article will think otherwise. Nevertheless, even for faithful churchgoers there are some facts about the significance of preaching that need an airing.

First of all, let's be clear that I am writing about the sermon as the formal proclamation of the Gospel delivered within the context of Christian worship by an accredited minister. The sermon thus defined is one ingredient in a carefully constructed and traditional pattern of worship, which includes prayer, praise and sacrament, and is a pattern which reaches back to the dawn of Christianity. Throughout Church history, and across the denominations, the sermon has varied greatly in prominence. At one end of the scale it might be virtually non-existent or just a very brief homily, as in a quiet celebration of the service of Holy Communion. At the other end, it could almost assume the expansive proportions attributed by W.S. Gilbert in "The Mikado" to those "mystical Germans who preach from ten till four." At all events, the sermon is not the same as an address, or a talk, or a eulogy.

I cannot help thinking of the awesome responsibility of the Christian preacher. Their task has been summarised by one astute commentator as being "to comfort the afflicted and afflict the comfortable". That's a very good working description of the aim and objective of a sermon. It is certainly in line with the ministry of Jesus who cared so much about those who were hurting, and challenged so forcefully the self-satisfied establishment. A Christian preacher must constantly be looking for ways of proclaiming the Good News (Gospel) of salvation while at the same time having the boldness to speak uncomfortable truths in the manner of the biblical prophets. This he must do even at the risk of becoming unpopular, even reviled.[4] A sermon is not for entertainment, and a preacher is not

---

[4]   Let me say at this point that I am using the masculine pronoun to avoid the awkwardness of
      repeatedly having to write 'he/she' but of course my remarks apply to preachers of either gender.

called by God in order to display skills in oratory, or to demonstrate his erudition, or to share his favourite prejudices or air his private opinions on public matters. Yet he must aim to be compelling, eloquent, confident, knowledgeable (especially about the Bible) as well as prayerful. He must feel deeply the urge to express the love of God and to proclaim the Good News of Jesus crucified and risen. He must also be relevant and sensitive to the needs and nature of the congregation whom he is called to serve in ministry.

## Responsibility

This opens up many avenues to explore which cannot be entered here. So I now focus on one issue that tends to be forgotten, especially in these days of informal approaches and the general loosening up of relations between clergy and parishioners. That is the question of Authority. Preaching the Word of God is a weighty responsibility. To balance this, the preacher who has been called to the ordained or lay (Reader) ministry has been unambiguously given the *authority* to carry out this task. This is made clear when the Bishop presents him with a Bible at the ceremony of Ordination or Licensing. The old (1662) wording in the service sums it up succinctly: "Take thou Authority (with a capital 'A') to preach the Word of God." Whatever any worshipper thinks of the preacher or the sermon (and who doesn't!), the Minister of the Word has the spiritual authority to do what he must do, for better or for worse.

Every preacher must, of course, exercise this authority only after careful and continuing study and prayer, for he is to speak in God's name and not on his own whim. This is why ministers need regularly to spend time away from the pastoral coalface for reflection, prayer and study. Importantly, this is also a compelling reason why every sermon should begin with the declaration "In the Name of God, the Father, the Son and the Holy Spirit." In addition, a text from the Bible should customarily be used. This is partly to indicate where the preacher's authority derives from, and partly to focus the minds of both the preacher and the congregation.

In this regard, I have a vivid recollection when, about fifty years ago, I happened to be sitting in the congregation in Tewkesbury Abbey fairly near the front, one row behind an elderly lady. When the young curate went into the pulpit for the sermon, to my surprise the lady took out from her bag a small collapsible ear trumpet made of tortoiseshell and put it to her ear, aiming it at the preacher. In place of a Bible text, the preacher began "I wonder how many of you have seen those witty jokes on the back of matchboxes." At that point, the lady removed the ear trumpet and instantly closed it with a very audible SNAP. If you have ever experienced the resonance in Tewkesbury Abbey, you will appreciate how the lady (who must have sat in that pew since the days of the curate's grandparents) had eloquently expressed her opinion about modern styles of preaching!

The ending of the sermon is important too. Traditionally, after drawing to a close, the preacher would say a very brief prayer usually referring to the authority of God, "to whom, as is justly due, belongs all might, majesty, authority and power", ending, of course, with "Amen" (so be it). So with the sermon being spiritually authoritative, it is *not* appropriate to conclude a liturgical sermon with a formula such as "Thank you for listening." A Christian congregation does not need to be thanked for listening to a sermon because the congregation is part of the shared liturgical process of hearing and responding to the Word of God. That is what the worshippers are there for: they are simply carrying out their spiritual duty. Worshippers are, of course, free, outside the context of the liturgy (i.e. when the service is over or at some other time) to comment, criticise, disagree or discuss the sermon, and every preacher should encourage and welcome such responses. Perhaps in this respect, the last word might go with the faithful worshipper who wisely remarked "Well, you can always learn *something* from a sermon, even if it is only patience!"

## Postscript

From what I have said, it should be clear that these remarks do not refer to an "address", or a "talk", or even evangelistic preaching, events which take place during informal worship, at meetings, or out in the streets. In this article I am only concerned about the sermon as part of a formal liturgical act of worship, which, in the case of the Anglican Church, could be The Holy Communion (Eucharist), Morning Prayer or Evening Prayer, or the Offices of Baptism, Marriage and Funeral.

Now here's an interesting postscript on the significance of an introductory biblical text. This event happened during the first half of the 20th century. A newly ordained young curate was due to preach his first sermon in the church in Cheltenham to which he had been appointed at the start of his ministry. He was recovering from the flu, but more than this, he was also suffering from extreme nervousness at the coming ordeal, for the church was well attended, and family and friends were also there for the occasion. When he got to the pulpit, he was sweating profusely and in such a state of nerves that he only managed to declaim his Bible text before he collapsed completely and had to be carried out.

Years later, after many years of successful ministry in various parishes, this priest was vicar of a large and prestigious church in the North of England. One Sunday morning after the service, he was greeting members of the congregation at the church door. One of them was a complete stranger to him, and as he shook hands, the man said "We have actually met before. Do you remember your first sermon?" The vicar chuckled. "How could I ever forget it! I never got beyond the text." The stranger then came out with an extraordinary remark: "That sermon changed my life", he said. And he meant it in all seriousness. The Word of God in that text, perhaps fortified by the circumstances in which it was spoken, had made a deep spiritual impact in the life of at least one member of that Cheltenham congregation so many years before.

⸻⟨◦⟩⸻

# The Sorcerer's Apprentice

Solihull Parish Magazine October 2018

Mickey Mouse came to life in 1928, three years before I was born. Unlike me, he hasn't aged at all! When I was nine, he featured in a Walt Disney film called "Fantasia". Disney chose eight pieces of classical music and skilfully matched them with animation, creating an entertainment which was an instant success and delighted audiences for many years. The scene which most successfully caught the imagination of all age groups was "The Sorcerer's Apprentice" in which Mickey Mouse stars in the leading role. It is still popular and you can watch it on YouTube. The catchy music, by the French composer Paul Dukas, was written in 1887. He was inspired by the poem *The Sorcerer's Apprentice* written by the German poet Goethe one hundred years earlier.

The story is comic. While the magician is absent, his lazy apprentice seizes the opportunity to use one of his master's spells to enchant a broom. The idea was to get the broom to relieve him of the onerous task of carrying buckets from a fountain to fill a bath with water. Unfortunately, he cannot find the spell to stop the process, so the bath overflows and a stupendous flood ensues. The hapless apprentice splits the broom with an axe, only to find that there are now two brooms doubling the disaster, and the whole situation gets totally out of hand. Fortunately, the sorcerer returns in time to put everything in order again.

It is interesting to note that Goethe was looking back to similar stories of unintended mayhem, which were popular in the Middle Ages. Scholars have even found a comparable tale in Greek literature of the first century AD. So it seems that, as with many fairy tales and nursery rhymes, the Sorcerer's Apprentice story is touching on some basic idea about human behaviour.

If that is the case, then behind the fun and comedy there is a serious message that we need to take notice of, because it could be relevant to our own time and situation. For example, while I was once again crawling irritatingly between five and ten miles an hour along a road built for vehicles to travel up to 70 m.p.h. it occurred to me that somebody's magic spells had gone badly wrong. The clever technology which had created motor cars and put them within the reach of millions, together with roads on which you can drive them safely at speed, has produced exactly the opposite effect, so that we are now on the verge of a crisis in traffic management. I could go on about the electronic/digital revolution, which has given us the blessings (?) of computers, instant communication, and social media, but I won't. There could hardly be a better example of human ingenuity creating a situation that is rapidly getting out of control.

In the old story, the sorcerer's apprentice made two serious mistakes:

- he thought only of his own personal comfort (magically getting the broom to do his work for him while the magician was away)
- he forgot that he was only an apprentice, not a magician.

The analogy holds good in the human situation. And when you come to think of it, on one level the whole of Scripture contains a record of these two human errors:

- self-centred detachment from the Divine Source or Sorcerer (the cat's away so the mickey mouses can play!)
- a tragic misunderstanding and misuse of power.

In the Old Testament, there is trouble every time the rulers and others fail to follow the Divine Will, and the legend of Adam and Eve acts as a stark backdrop to this drama. In the New Testament, both the teaching and the destiny of Jesus witness to the same state of affairs: for instance, the prodigal son 'doing his own thing' and ending up devouring pig-swill, or the estate workers who attempt violently to take over the estate during the absence of the owner (Luke 15 and 20). And of course, the crucifixion of total innocence is a prime example of the wonkiness of human power structures.

It is also important to note the connection which the Bible makes between human action and the environment, whether this is seen in terms of the droughts, floods or pests in the Old Testament, or the chilling disasters seen by John in his Revelation dream. Mickey Mouse unwittingly causes a flood by misusing a magic spell. Consider what sort of mayhem can ensue if or when human beings allow unbridled use of atomic energy or digital technology with scant, if any, reference to the Love-Wisdom-Power of God.

It is as well that we should remember that in this life, and in God's eyes, we are apprentices, not sorcerers.

**St Peter's Church Alstonefield**

You may be forgiven for not knowing where Alstonefield is. I certainly didn't until I came across it by chance, not far from Ashbourne in Derbyshire, when I was enjoying a solitary walking tour in that part of the Peak District National Park. The quintessentially beautiful English village with its medieval church is just one of a host of lovely and interesting places to see in that area.

This two-decker pulpit is similar to the one from which I preached my first sermon in Castle Bromwich in 1961. The Puritan influence after the Reformation led to a strong emphasis being placed on sermons, and pulpits like this, as well as even more elaborate three-deckers, appeared in many English churches during the 18$^{th}$ and early 19$^{th}$ centuries. Should you find yourself in Chichester, there is a spectacular sample in the redundant church of St John the Evangelist. This is what Wikipedia has to say about it:

*It has been called the best surviving three-decker pulpit in Sussex. An unusual refinement of the more common two-decker structure, a three-decker allowed different parts of the service to be read from different levels according to their importance. Responses to prayers were read from the lowest deck, usually by the church clerk. The main part of the service, including prayers, came from the middle deck; and the sermon—the most important part of a Low church service—took place in the circular upper deck ... The three sections are now side by side, but originally they were aligned one in front of the other in a tiered formation.*

That's one up on Alstonefield (and Castle Bromwich. However, Alstonefield churchyard contains the oldest legible gravestone in the country: so there!

⋯◇⋯

# The spiritual health service
### Solihull Parish Magazine October 2013 (revised)

During the 1960s I attended a healing service in Birmingham Cathedral. The officiant and preacher was the Revd. George Bennett, then a hospital chaplain. I was among those who received from him the ministry of the laying on of hands. A few years later I was to have the privilege of sharing that ministry with him at Crowhurst, the home of healing in Sussex, with which he was to become closely associated. Following the service in our Cathedral, I became convinced that the Church should never neglect to share in the healing work of Jesus, not by performing miracles which were special to him, but by recognising in positive ways that human illness and malaise are deeply connected with the spiritual dimension of people's lives.

Medical skill and psychological understanding are of great importance; without the insights of modern medicine I should not be here today writing this article. However, for true healing/health/wholeness we must have some understanding of our connectedness with God who is the 'author and giver of all good things' (BCP Collect), including the expertise of the medical and caring professions.

The reason why the National Health Service seems doomed to move from one crisis to another is because this truth is not sufficiently understood or recognised. As long as practitioners and patients alike are detached from the spiritual dimension of healing, oblivious of the hand of God at work at every level of sickness and health, then the whole operation is in danger of collapse. It will become little more than a health factory doling out increasingly expensive cures for symptoms, a situation that is clearly not sustainable. The recent move to deprive hospitals of their chaplaincies is itself a symptom of this trend.

## Your Church

We do well not to pay too much attention to the miraculous side of the Jesus story. As George Bennett used to say, "Jesus couldn't help healing". This was not simply because he had a special gift (which he obviously did have), it was because he could see beyond the visible symptoms of the sufferers and into the spiritual needs of the individuals and the society of which they were a part. So, for example, he was not afraid to point out the connection between sickness and sin, nor to challenge the chronically sick with such a question as "Do you want to be healed?"

The local Church, ideally, should be a therapeutic community, caring and healing in the name of Jesus. After all, the Church has a long tradition of continuing the healing ministry of Jesus. This begins in the earliest years as the New Testament clearly shows, not so much in the performing of spectacular miracles, as in the building of small faith communities comprised of a disparate collection of people prepared to reconcile their differences and care for one another in the name of Jesus and for the love of God: male, female, Jew, Greek, Roman, Parthian, Mede, Elamite etc. Ever since then, the Christian Church has exercised a healing ministry in all kinds of ways down the centuries, with monasteries playing a key role in this respect. The widespread provision of health facilities today rests firmly on the foundation of such work.

What is required in the Church now is not high-profile miracles, but a continuing of the patient groundwork of prayer and intercession, backing up the more frontline ministry of sacramental healing such as anointing and the laying on of hands. At the same time we need to encourage, and carefully monitor, any special gifts of healing that there might be among church members. Along with these ongoing tasks, there needs to be a much stronger prophetic voice proclaiming the need for repentance and reconciliation in our society, which is spiritually sick and very much in need of God's healing grace.

—————<o>—————

# Violence: civil disorder from a Biblical perspective

### Solihull Parish Magazine February 2012

Although it was first published in 2012, this article was written following the London riots during August 2011. They began in Tottenham in London and then, in copycat fashion, spread to other major cities including Birmingham. The riots may be part of history now, but I believe that what I wrote then is still relevant.

It was something of a challenge when I was recently asked to preach on the Epistle to the Hebrews: not the most straightforward text in the New Testament by any means. It was even more of a challenge to do so on the Sunday in August which followed the most serious rioting, looting and public disorder experienced in living memory on the streets of some of our cities. My text came from the closing words of the Epistle: "May the God of peace, who brought back from the dead our Lord Jesus, the great Shepherd of the sheep, through the blood of an eternal covenant, make you perfect in all goodness so that you may do his will." Simply to remind the congregation that, in Christian teaching, God is a God of peace, seemed to me to be a good starting point. There are many in the world who live their lives in the service of a God of war. And there are plenty more who, professing no belief in God, are dedicated to violence, or indifferent to it, or just totally bemused by it and want to bury their heads in the sand.

Following the August riots, questions were asked about the causes. Most of the answers that people gave were superficial. We desperately want to find somebody to blame: parents, schools, the government, the "cuts", the media. Some people voiced the opinion that we are all, to some extent, responsible for the society in which we live and which we have created. That is nearer the truth. The real truth of the matter, however, lies much deeper. The seeds of the troubles in August were sown in the 19th and 20th centuries.

Consider, first of all, the main targets of the rioters: shops and the police. It seems to have gone unnoticed that, ten years ago, the prime targets in the 9/11 tragedy in the USA were the World Trade Centre and the Pentagon. Trade and Authority – we have here a meaningful parallel. Since the 1960s it has been the chief concern of wealthier developed countries to enhance trade and encourage consumerism. Enormous global corporations have been set up to do this in complete disregard of the growing depth of poverty among the less well-off nations. By means of clever marketing techniques, we in the richer countries have been carefully groomed to extend, to an unprecedented degree, the list of material things (including food) that we have come to believe we cannot do without. In our part of the world, there are more, and fuller, shops than there have ever been. Shopping, mostly for inessentials, appears to be the most popular leisure pastime.

**Unemployment**
Tied in with this is the apparent total inability of successive governments in the industrialised nations, over the past 100 years, to do anything about unemployment, short of waging war. Rioters and looters come mainly from the ranks of the unemployed. Since the ending of National Service in 1963, no viable alternatives have been found for dealing imaginatively, on a nationwide scale, with the natural energies and dynamism of young men. The provision of post-16 education in colleges and universities is of little consequence if there is nothing for young adults to do later on. We know that sterling work has been done by voluntary agencies since the 1950s, principally churches, in running clubs and other organisations for young people. Governmental support for this, however, has been paltry, and no consistent visionary thinking has been happening in the field of youth employment and leisure.

My reading from the Epistle to the Hebrews began: "Obey your leaders and submit to their authority" (13.17). Here is a conundrum. When leaders in commerce, media, finance, and politics are primarily self-serving and found to be corrupt, we cannot expect the general public to have respect for symbols of authority, whether the Pentagon or the police.

Behind all this lies the root cause, which I believe is spiritual. The 19th century saw the start of a major shift from belief in God. Atheism and secularism within the industrialised countries led to the dramatic decline in Christian religious observance that we experienced during the 20th century. Unfortunately, Christians also tended to collude with consumerist policies and thus lost the ability to challenge effectively the secular and materialist society of which they found themselves a part. A sizeable proportion of people in the developed world now assume (falsely) that they can manage their lives, and often the lives of other people, without reference to God. The consequences of this detachment from the Divine Source are clearly spelt out in the Bible, principally by the Old Testament prophets and the book Deuteronomy (and in dramatically symbolic terms in the Book of Revelation). The connection between God-forgetfulness and violence is interpreted by the prophets as God's judgment on the nation. However, beyond the more extreme evangelical wings of Christianity, such matters are rarely raised by Christian teachers and preachers.

**Innovative**
The causes of our current problems are deep-seated, and therefore the solutions cannot be short term. To begin with, religious people of all faiths will need to find a deeper holiness of life, paying more serious attention to prayer. They will also have to find new and innovative ways of bringing their non-religious friends and neighbours to an understanding of their personal need to link with God. Political and business leaders will have to pay far more attention to the spiritual needs of young people, as well as to their own standards of integrity. They will need to be reminded that they are gifted and called to serve others rather than to pursue the mirage of success and feather their own nests in the process. Those who study and manipulate the economies of the nations must find imaginative and, perhaps, ground-breaking ways of managing wealth, which do not inevitably keep people out of work.

All this will not happen in the short term. As things are, we are likely to experience further violent disturbance, both locally and globally. But that decidedly does not mean that we lose heart or the will to work for change. My text from Hebrews reminds us that the God of peace is alive and active: also that he "brought back from the dead our Lord Jesus", a real resurrection from hopelessness and despair. This living Jesus is described as "the great Shepherd of the sheep", which in Biblical terms means the ultimate reference point for all true leadership. The Church's task is to persist in making these things known by every possible means.

# Word of the Lord
## Solihull Parish Magazine December 2014

In my younger days, when we read the Bible in church, we used to say at the end of the reading, "Here ends (or endeth) the first (or second) lesson." Then the new forms of service came along towards the end of the last century, and we were expected to say at the end of our reading, "This is the Word of the Lord." I ask, "Why?"

As often as not, what I have just read is not the Word of the Lord: it is the word of St. Paul, or the word of an evangelist, or the word of a prophet, or of an unknown historian or commentator in ancient Israel. If, as sometimes happens, you are reading an extract from the Old Testament which consists of a vivid account of battle and bloodshed, murder and mayhem, it seems nonsensical to conclude it by declaring to the congregation that "this is the Word of the Lord".

The explanation that is normally given for using this formula is simply to say that the Bible is the Word of God, and leave it at that. This is a cop-out which neatly sidesteps the necessity to think creatively about the Scriptures. There is no question that the Scriptures handed down to us are inspired, which is to say that they are breathed into (in-spired) by the Spirit of God to such an extent that they carry Divine authority and deserve to be read, studied, taken seriously and prayed over. But to use a formula which simply says "BIBLE = GOD'S WORD" actually damages that authority by limiting the Word of God to written texts.

In fact, the Bible itself testifies in the strongest possible terms that The Word of God is something far broader, deeper and more significant than a collection of handwritten documents, however ancient and venerable such documents may be. Consider these texts:

*By the Word of the Lord were the heavens made.*   Ps. 33.6
*By faith we understand that the worlds have been framed by the Word of God.*
Heb. 11.3
*In the Beginning was the Word ... and the Word was made flesh.*
John 1.1 & 14
*He sustains all things by his powerful Word.*  Hebrews 1.3
*Man(kind) lives by every Word that proceeds from the mouth of God.*
Luke 4.4 (Deut 8.3)

*You shall put these Words of mine into you heart and soul.* Deut 11.18
*My Words shall never pass away.* Mark 13.31
*My Words are Spirit and Life.* John 6.63

This, then, is "the Word of the Lord." The Word is not just an extract from a sacred text, selected to be read within the confines of a sacred building. The Word of God encompasses the whole of the created order, from the outermost galaxy to the innermost atomic particle. The Word is the Self-expression of the ineffable God who is above all and in all. The Word is the outworking of salvation through Jesus-Messiah-Christ who is the Word-made-flesh.

This is awesome, and might well lead us to a loss of words: for the most appropriate response to such a majestic scenario would indeed be silence. How can one express the inexpressible!

Yet I dare to add one further thought regarding the Bible as the Word of God. In the broad context of the Grand Design, our Holy Scriptures are certainly of great significance as a divinely inspired (i.e Spirit-filled) revelation of God. Taken as a whole, the Bible is not so much the Word of God as a vessel that contains speech from God. Like priceless jewels in a rich setting, many Sayings that command attention shine out from the text. They are God speaking in the First Person, words that are transmitted through his holy prophets, or through angelic messengers, or supremely through Jesus. They may be encouraging, or comforting, or challenging, or critical, or they may convey some vital spiritual truth. They may be spoken to individuals, or to groups, or to a nation, but they are relevant to humanity as a whole from generation to generation. They require close attention, and they are best listened to in contemplative silence before being acted upon. Here are a few of the many hundreds to be found in the Bible:

| | |
|---|---|
| Abide in me as I abide in you. | John 15.4 |
| If you seek ME with all your heart, I will let you find ME. | Jeremiah 29.13 |
| I am [. . . ] the living one [. . .] alive for evermore. | Revelation 1.18 |
| Ye shall be holy, for I the Lord your God am holy. | Leviticus 19.2 |
| I am the bread of life [. . .] which I will give [. . .] for the life of the world. | John 6. 48.51 |

I [...] hold you by the right hand [...] do not be
afraid, I will help you.                                    Isaiah 41.13
You shall bear witness for me                              Acts 1.8

These and many more Sayings can be found with brief commentaries in
my book "Within Thy Silence".

# You, me, and John the Baptist
Mike's Musings June 2007

Every now and then through the year, the gaunt and challenging figure of
John the Baptist emerges from the pages of the Bible, and moves across
the Church's calendar. His feast day, 24 June, is midsummer. The days are
long; the weather is warm, or it should be. Perhaps we can be forgiven if
we don't take as much notice as we should of this stentorian prophetic
voice, which summons us to repent. Just to make sure, we get a reminder
in Advent. So, whether in June or December, I suggest that we listen more
attentively to the voice from the wilderness – "prepare the way of the
Lord".

What an astonishing figure he was, and what an impact he made! That
is hardly surprising, seeing that such a prophet had not been seen in Israel
for 400 years or more. And what charisma! The people flocked to hear
him; he called them "a brood of vipers" and they came back for more. It
is interesting that his desert ministry started a movement that continued
long after his death. I think that, in the first century, this Baptist movement
was actually more successful in the early stages than Christianity. You can
find followers of John popping up here and there in first-century documents, including the Acts of the Apostles, chapters 18 and 19.

Jesus took the Baptist and his message very seriously. In fact, when he
began his ministry, Jesus even borrowed some of John's sermons. For
example, we hear him preaching, like John, "repent, for the kingdom of
heaven is at hand" (Mark 1.14). Then, of course, we find Jesus branching
out in a different direction – a hands-on ministry of compassion and

healing in parallel with the preaching and teaching. This was the actual coming-into-existence of the long-awaited "day of the Lord" which the prophets had foretold.

## News – good and bad

One of the keynotes of Jesus's ministry was the conveying of good news to people who were underprivileged and marginalized. "Tell John (said Jesus) that the poor are receiving the good news" (Matthew 11. 5). John's preaching was important, and one of its features was that the more privileged people in society who came to hear him actually heard, not good news, but bad. That is to say, they were told in no uncertain terms where they had got things wrong. Jesus wasn't afraid to do that either ("woe to you, scribes and Pharisees"). And here is a clear message for the Church in any age, including our own. The task is laid on Christian people, especially leaders, to point out where those who are privileged can so easily go wrong.

It is said that the task of the Christian preacher is "to afflict the comfortable, and to comfort the afflicted." We are reasonably good at the second part, but not nearly so good at the first. There is a good deal of comforting and caring going on, both within and beyond Christianity. In fact, people and organisations far beyond the Church have taken many leaves out of the Christian book in this respect. Millions of pounds are raised for charity and aid. And the afflicted are being comforted in all kinds of ways. But we need to ask the question: "Are the comfortable being afflicted by the Word of God?" If not, then many of the root causes of affliction in the world are being ignored. Millions may be poured into charity, but is there, in fact, more justice for the poor as a result? The question hangs in the air.

## Spiritual treasures

Judgment, retribution, and the wrath of God on one hand – healing, restoration and peace on the other. The bad news, and the good. Both elements are there in the Gospel, and the Bible, as usual, paints the picture in black and white. We, however, look at the scene through the prism of faith, and we see many colours. Sometimes it is confusing, trying to sort out the good from the bad, the comforts from the afflictions, the saints from the sinners. But both sorts of messages are needed, and we need to take note of both John the Baptist and of Jesus.

That gaunt figure of the Baptist, clothed in skins and living on locusts, stalks through our shopping centres and peers into our wardrobes and supermarket trolleys. "The kingdom of heaven is close at hand," he says, "think about it!"

So, too, does Jesus nudge us, more gently perhaps, but yet very firmly, with the good news of that same kingdom. We must pay attention to it, and share it with the world. "The kingdom of God is within you," is his message, at least in part (Luke 17. 21). The things that matter, God's peace, God's joy, God's love, are to be found not in outward show, but in the quiet places of the heart. It is only those who take the trouble truly to seek these spiritual treasures who will find them. And it is only those who find them and embrace them, who have the ability, or the authority, to share that peace and joy and love with those who (in the words of the Prayer Book) "are in any ways afflicted or distressed". That is our Christian agenda, drawn up for us by both Jesus and John the Baptist.

**Bourton On The Hill**

As I was driving one day in the Cotswolds, this caught my eye. I just had to stop the car, cross the field and draw it, without knowing in the least what it was. It seemed a bit like a Calvary. The arms pivoted on the uprights so that they could swivel in the breeze. Enquiries led to the sculptor Andrew Darke. I sent him a copy of my sketch and he responded kindly:

*The piece is called "Cleaved Air" and is so called partly because of the cleaving process I used to make it and, of course, because the cleaved pieces cleave the air, so to speak, as it [sic] moves. The uprights are made of oak and the cross pieces cleaved from sweet chestnut which is a lighter timber and one of the best for cleaving. You catch the piece quite nicely in your sketch and I'm pleased to have the copy.*

Andrew is a member of PLACE, a group of artists and others who are passionately concerned about the detrimental visual impact that modern infrastructures such as wind farms, pylons, and mobile phone masts make on the environment. They make this statement on their website:

*Most people are familiar with the concept of endangered species. We believe there are also endangered experiences. An empty sky, for instance, or the dark of the night sky unaffected by manufactured light, both of which would have been common experiences in the relatively recent past, have all but disappeared.*

*Spatial freedom in landscapes clear of human structures is ever more rare in the British Isles. Absolute aloneness is difficult to find. A sense of the frailty and inconsequence of human life when immersed in the vastness of the elements, gives a much needed and powerful change of perspective. We believe that humanity is diminished by the ongoing loss of such experiences. Many of these losses are unnecessary.*

# PART TWO

# Themes and Variations

# CHAPTER ONE

# *Resurrection*

## Alive, Alive, O!
Solihull Parish News April 2014

A recent event has caused me to think deeply once again about how modern society understands death. A friend in his eighties was dying. We'll call him "Clive" (not his real name). He was a churchgoing Christian and he had accepted that his illness was terminal. His hospital treatment had not been able to effect any cure or amelioration of his condition and he had decided to be discharged so that he could die at home. During the last conversation I had with him, we chatted openly and contentedly about his funeral arrangements.

A short time passed. Then Clive developed an eating problem, and his doctor advised that he should go for an endoscopy to investigate if anything could be done to relieve the situation: a day job at the local hospital. But after being seen by a specialist, he was immediately connected up to life support machinery, something that was patently against his wishes. The family were powerless to prevent this. During the next few days the family spent many hours at the bedside, during which time Clive was seldom conscious. It was while they had, of necessity, to take a few hours respite that they got a phone call to say that he had died, alone.

Now, here is a quotation taken from a letter that the young Mozart wrote to his father:

*Since death is the true goal of our lives, I have made myself so well acquainted during the last few years with this true and best friend of mankind that the idea of it no longer has any terrors for me, but rather much that is tranquil and comforting. And I thank God that he has granted me the good fortune to obtain the opportunity of regarding death as the key to our true happiness. I never lie down in my bed without considering that, young as I am, perhaps I may on the morrow be no more. Yet not one of those who know me could say that I am morose or melancholy, and for this I thank my Creator daily, and wish heartily that the same happiness may be given to my fellow-men.*

Reading that, I am reminded strongly of the verse in St Francis' hymn of creation:

*And thou, most kind and gentle death,*
*Waiting to hush our latest breath,*
*O praise Him; Alleluia!*
*Thou leadest home the child of God,*
*And Christ the Lord the way hath trod;*
*O praise Him; Alleluia!*

What a contrast those words are to the general attitude towards dying and death which is prevalent in our society today. The most common view is quite the opposite, in which death is considered to be our worst and most dreaded enemy. Often, and especially in hospitals, death is frequently seen as nothing other than a clinical failure, a tragedy, an event to be shielded from, something to be avoided as far as possible, a topic not to be discussed, especially in front of children. The general trend is that people must be kept alive at all costs (literally whatever the cost), regardless of their age or the severity of their illness.

The words from Mozart's letter are quoted in a book published in 2010 by Jennifer Worth, author of the now famous TV series "Call the Midwife." Entitled "In the Midst of Life", the book is principally about the vexed issue of resuscitation. It contains some horrific stories of people being kept clinically alive when common sense can plainly see that death would be the better option. It also picks its way, in expert and sensitive fashion, through the tangled undergrowth of the law, medical ethics, together with matters of faith and human emotions. This book would make profitable reading for all who are engaged in the medical and caring professions, as well as all Christian ministers, ordained and lay.

One might expect that among Christians, who profess an Easter faith, there would be a strong body of opinion to counteract the prevailing negative attitude surrounding the inevitable end of our earthly life. Sadly this is by no means the case. Over fifty years in Christian ministry has taught me that far too many Christians accept without question that dying is a gruesome business which is mainly the province of medics, and that death is nothing but a tragedy, a loss, and a cause for gloom and sorrow. It seems that, on this topic, the Church has lost its nerve and sold out to a non-Christian, non-Biblical way of thinking which considers this life as all there is, and which has little or no hope of resurrection and beyond.

A true Christian faith has Easter at its apex, and our New Testament bears the strongest possible witness to this. In the light of this, a Christian's attitude to dying and death should encourage others to consider dying and death, not as a painful black hole into which we are destined to drop, but as a platform on which we prepare for a new stage in our spiritual journey. The more strongly we hold on to our Easter faith, the more chance we shall have of challenging the uncomfortable gloominess and despair that so often prevails in the face of life's ending.

I end with a few quotes from Jenny Worth's book:

*'Let me bide, dears,' my grandfather said to his daughters a few days before his death. 'I want for nothing.' And they allowed him to die quietly. Most dying people seem to feel the same – the Angel of Death brings peace. Harassing a dying person to return to the life they have already left is a pointless exercise, and in many instances, cruel.*

*'Hope is not the conviction that something will turn out well, but the certainty that something makes sense, regardless of how it turns out.' (V.Haval, playwright and President of the Czech Republic)*

*Those who have been close to the dying and seen death in all its awesome mystery can get a glimpse of what it is about, and even then only a glimpse. The whole picture includes a spiritual dimension. God is not in the churches, or the mosques or synagogues. He resides not in temples and minarets. God is not the possession of priests or rabbis or mullahs. God is at the deathbed, tenderly drawing the living soul from the dying body. God is in the grief and suffering of those who are left behind. . . If we can find no spirituality in life, death is an uncomfortable reminder of a missing dimension.*

*The social taboo surrounding death is deep-seated, and it is most unhealthy. How has it developed? . . . I have a theory that it started after the First World War when 8? million young men worldwide died in battle, when 21 million were maimed or mutilated and when upwards of 40 million died in the flu epidemic of 1918. And the carnage didn't end there. The bloodiest century in history killed up to half a billion men, women and children. Everyone was so sickened by death and loss and grieving that perhaps they just couldn't take any more. So they turned their backs, and thus started the climate of denial that inhibits us to this day.*

*It is well nigh impossible to talk to anyone about death, I find. Most people seem deeply embarrassed. It is like when I was a girl and nobody could talk about sex. We all did it, but nobody talked about it! We have now grown out of that silly taboo, and we must grow out of our inhibitions surrounding death. They have arisen largely because so few people see death any more, even though it is quite obviously in our midst. A cultural change must come, a new atmosphere of freedom, which will only happen if we open our closed minds.*

—◇—

# Death is ...
## Solihull Parish News April 2014

There is, I hope, a corner in Purgatory (not in Heaven) where we can have an opportunity to express in appropriate yet robust terms our feelings about some of things that irritate us most: and I hope that it can be arranged, where possible, that the people who have caused those things will be able to overhear what we say. I would like the chance to berate Frank Sinatra for having sung *My Way* – surely a prime example of the worst kind of egoistic self-congratulation, or in traditional Christian language, of the sin of Pride. And I am longing to commiserate with Henry Scott-Holland. How he must wring his hands in despair hearing a fragment of his splendid sermon on death torn out of context and reduced to sentimental clap-trap at funerals, "Death is nothing at all".[5]

Both these monstrous distortions of what it means to be truly human have unfortunately become regular accompaniments to a crematorium funeral. I now know, after many years of contacts with the un-churched bereaved, that when they request *My Way* to be played at the funeral, this is in most cases a clear indication that the deceased person had been a sore trial to his family – self-centred, aggressive, and determined to have things 'his way' regardless of the pain or inconvenience that he caused to other people (yes; it seems always to be for a man that they ask for *My Way*).

---

[5]  The sermon which contains these words was preached by Henry Scott-Holland at the lying-in-state of King Edward VII in 2010. Read it in full on the Internet. That will set the record straight.

Where, in the words of that song, will you find anything of true humanity – of courtesy, of generosity, of friendliness, of self-sacrifice, of outgoing love and compassion, beauty and joy? The answer is, 'nowhere'.

The Scott-Holland fragment is worse still. It is read out of context and consequently has become a sickly mask concealing even deeper spiritual falsehoods than the Sinatra song. It does something that the sermon definitely does not do: the words succeed in trivialising what is in fact one of the key significant spiritual events after birth. Death is very important and very significant. Like many other matters of human significance, death is characterised by enigma and paradox. Far from being "nothing at all", human death in any form is supremely mysterious, mystical and awesome. It may rightly be considered as tragic and terrible, "the last enemy" as St Paul calls it (1 Corinthians 15.25), for it destroys and separates, it creates suffering and sorrow, and it often has to take place in a context of pain or violence or following the sad decay of the physical body. On the other hand, death can be the bringer of peace after toil and anguish, the ultimate healer, an occasion of joy and thanksgiving, an opportunity for reconciliation and the renewal of faith, and an affirmation of the assurance of resurrection and salvation.

## Glory, wonder and power

In a recent article, Fr Rodney Hacking (an associate of the Community of the Servants of the Will of God) makes a plea for the positive statement of the faith and traditions of the Holy Catholic Church at the time of funeral to counteract the bland and almost meaningless social analgesic which is so often on offer at our sanitized crematoria. "It is [he writes] one of the tasks of the Catholic faith to save us from our native tendency to hide from the awe-fulness of death … It is boldness and confidence that we have to manifest in the face of death, not slush. These things, however, emerge from a willingness to be real about what death is. Death is scary: it terrifies me at times. I have seen many peaceful deaths and I would like to go like that. I have also seen people die in pain, distress and fear … and I can tell you that death is definitely not 'nothing at all'."

The Christian fabric of the meaning of death and the rites of funeral has been irreparably torn, Fr Hacking complains. "Increasingly funeral services have become essentially memorial services: favourite readings and music of the deceased, and some 'words' either from a relative or friend, or rapidly gleaned and repeated by the poor parson who never knew the deceased.

And we have gone along with this because, above all, we have wanted to be liked and we have liked to be wanted." He notes that it is a good many years since he heard anyone preach or teach about Purgatory or Judgement. "Purgatory has come down to us mediated through the warped confusions of a sick Protestantism, as much else of our anti-Roman history, and little wonder it is that we fail to grasp that above all it is a place of Love. Our Host there is Christ Himself ever drawing us on through healing and restoration towards the fullness for which we are made".

Fr Hacking makes a strong plea for the use of the Requiem Mass as the most appropriate and sensible ministry that the Church has to offer at the time of funeral. "Given that for most of us the one Reality we shall have to face after death is Judgement (and few things are more clearly described in Holy Scripture and the Creeds of the Church) there will be no more important thing that the Church Militant can do for the deceased than to muster its resources on their behalf. I do know that on the day of Judgement there are some pretty unpalatable things to be faced and if I am to throw myself on the mercy of the court I shall hope to be able to rely on the support of the living. That is what a Requiem Mass is for and what it does … It is tragic that we have forgotten the power of the Mass … I fear that 16th century reformers and late 20th century liturgical vandals alike have stripped the Church of its main weapon, reduced by the one to something purely subjective, by the other to the level of an entertainment … (But) the Mass is indeed full of glory, wonder and power, for it is the extension of Christ's sacrificial death and resurrection in space and time. It is no mere commemoration, no mere memorial, it is real power. And on the day of judgement it is upon the power of the Mass, of the reality of the cross and resurrection through its offering that I shall rely. I must tell you that I know this for certain, for I have seen with my own eyes its power over the troubled dead."

Concerning his own funeral, Fr Hacking asks that his coffin should be brought into church and left there overnight. I know from pastoral experience how meaningful it is to include this as part of the preparation for Christian burial. It should be noted that the funeral services in our new prayer book (Common Worship: Pastoral Services) provide for this pre-funeral rite as well as for a Requiem, together with other pre- and post-funeral ministries. It is important that those who look for a Christian funeral should consider carefully all these options, which are centred on the worshipping community and the church building. The crematorium is a sensible and practical alternative for burial, but it is not, for Christians, an alternative Church.

⸺◇⸺

# Resurrection and Life
### Solihull Parish News March 2016

Earlier this year (2014) I attended the funeral of an old friend of the family. Susan (not her real name) was diagnosed with a terminal illness. About four months later she died, quite peacefully, in a Midlands hospice. She was not a practicing Christian. Like so many people these days, she hovered somewhere between faith and agnosticism. She had been a conscientious teacher, and also a loving wife, mother and grandmother. She loved gardening, and since retirement she had offered her services as a voluntary helper for her favourite charity. Altogether, Susan was a nice person to know.

Although she was not a churchgoer, Susan had been visited a few times by the local vicar during her final illness, and it was he who officiated at the funeral. The crematorium was packed with a congregation representing most age groups. The service lasted about half an hour. At its end I was left with very deep mixed feelings compounded of frustration, sorrow, sadness, even spiritual deprivation and some anger, all very difficult to suppress. In that context, of course, I had no choice but to bottle it all in.

The service began with an over-long unscripted introduction by the priest, which was really a eulogy in outline. This was followed by another tribute, haltingly and tearfully delivered by a friend of Susan. The vicar then started another eulogy in praise of Susan, into which he inserted the reading from Ecclesiastes chapter 3 about there being a season for everything … "a time to be born, and a time to die" … etc. Then came a lengthy extempore prayer which essentially was a repeat of the tributes already given in the guise of a thanksgiving for Susan's life. The Lord's Prayer got a slot at the end. After that came the 'hymn' *Morning has broken*, and then the final (again extempore) words of committal.

Apart from the Lord's Prayer and the passage from Ecclesiastes, there was nothing of the Anglican Funeral Office, nor even from the ecumenical service book provided for crematorium chapels. There were no words from the New Testament, no mention of the Resurrection (actually Jesus was only mentioned twice, both times in the formula "through Jesus Christ our Lord"). There were no prayers for Susan, nor indeed for the mourners or anyone else. At the end we had to sit through a recorded rendering of an old love song performed by a tenor of yester-year while the family wept copiously in the front pews. The coffin remained in view as we left. This was virtually a non-Christian, humanist funeral, taken by a Church of England vicar in a suit.

## Mind-set

This chilling experience confirmed in me the opinion I hold about the Church's stance in carrying out its funeral ministry: namely, that increasingly during the past sixty years, the Church of England has lost its nerve with respect to teaching the New Testament doctrine on dying and death. Western society in general has developed a mind-set that refuses to accept dying and death as normal and natural procedures. They are not in general topics of conversation. Medically, terminal illness and death are considered to be clinical failures. When old people die, relatives look around for someone to blame.

The Church has colluded with society to a large extent. Church services of Funeral and Burial have become no more than services of "Celebration and Thanksgiving for the life of ... "(as commonly printed on orders of service). Back-to-front funerals have become increasingly common. This is when as few people as possible attend a brief private burial or cremation, then everyone goes to church for a memorial service with no coffin. Tributes and eulogies have largely replaced the sermon, with the result that the clear opportunity for preaching the Good News of the death and resurrection of Jesus is often set aside just when it is most needed. Ask yourself when you last heard at a funeral the words "sin", "forgiveness", or "judgement" included in a reading or prayer, or during the address (The Lord's Prayer excepted). Yet these are key components in New Testament teaching relating to dying and death.

A true Christian faith has Holy Week and Easter as its apex. The more strongly we hold on to our Easter faith, the more chance we shall have of challenging our Christian ministers boldly to proclaim the glorious message of Resurrection at a time when people most need to hear it.

**Coventry Cathedral**

I have to admit that it took me many years fully to appreciate Basil Spence's daring design for a new Coventry Cathedral: my fault entirely, not his. When I first saw it not long after its consecration in 1962, I tended to agree with the angry critic who said that it looked more like an ice-cream factory than a church. Gradually I began to recognise that this was a shallow and uneducated comment, quite unworthy of a structure that was not only architecturally inspiring but also held a deep and truly Christian spirituality for those with eyes to see, a mind to ponder, and a heart to feel.

My original sketch was in pencil. Then I made a photocopy so that I could colour it. I'm sorry that the spire of the old cathedral had to be lost in mist, but there wasn't room on the paper to get it all in. I think the original drawing is actually better, but the colours here show more successfully the architect's carefully conceived placing of the ancient and modern. Jacob Epstein's sculpture at the entrance is truly awesome. The archangel Michael triumphs over a partially defeated Lucifer. The model for Saint Michael was the famous ballet dancer Robert Helpmann. His discipline, poise, and controlled strength contrasts dramatically with a flabby Satan in futile defiance. The whole piece eloquently proclaims the sublime Christian truth of the ultimate triumph of God over evil.

# CHAPTER TWO

# *Lent to the Lord*

## Borrowed Time
### Solihull Parish News March 2017

It has become common knowledge, and a regular (perhaps tediously regular) topic of conversation, that we are living longer. Very often these days the discussion centres around the growing pressure on the NHS trying to cope with an ageing population. I must admit that, during the years since I passed my biblically allotted "threescore years and ten" (Psalm 90, v 10), there has been a startling increase in my visits to the surgery, a place that I frequented but rarely before my 70th birthday.

Today, most of us expect to have a longer life than our grandparents. If someone dies in their seventies people often say "that was no great age." In my funeral and bereavement ministry, I was sometimes disturbed when excessive grief was shown by relatives of someone who died in their nineties, especially when this grief was accompanied by a stinging attack on the medical services for not keeping the person alive longer.

Now I want to make a remark about longevity that will probably raise a few eyebrows. I maintain that those of us who live beyond the age of forty are living on borrowed time. If you consider the whole history of humanity on our planet, it is only during the 20th century that we have thought of the age of forty as being young to middle-aged. In the 19th and earlier centuries, I reckon that most people over the age of forty would reckon they were approaching old age. If you use the Internet, go to the website *ourworldindata*, then search for *Life Expectancy*. You will find a fascinating collection of graphs and commentaries. Astonishingly, in spite of the inequalities in the world economies that we all know about, the average global life expectancy in 2015 was 70 years. But you only have to turn the pages of history back to 1850 to discover that, at that time, the overwhelming majority of the world's population could not expect to live much beyond 40. So it could be a salutary exercise to reflect on my assertion that anyone over the age of forty is living on borrowed time. On that basis, I could say that I myself have been cluttering up our planet during the past 45 years!

## Symbolic

As a student of the Bible and as a Christian, I find these thoughts extremely interesting if somewhat disturbing. Another Psalm (95, BCP version) ends with the words: "Forty years long was I grieved with this generation and said, 'It is a people that do err in their hearts, for they have not known my ways: unto whom I sware in my wrath that they should not enter into my rest.'" In the Bible, the number 40 crops up in various places: notably the number of years that Israel wandered in the wilderness between Egypt and the Promised Land before the Divine Sat Nav told them 'You have reached your destination' (Numbers 14.33): the number of days that Noah spent with his floating zoo on the flood waters (Genesis 6.4): the number of years there was peace in Israel during the time of the Judges (Judges 3.11, 5.31): the age of the cripple healed by Peter (Acts 4.22): and of course the number of days Jesus spent in the wilderness after his baptism being tested (tempted) by the devil (Luke 4.1-13).

The fact is that the number 40 is symbolic. It actually stands for a lifetime. In biblical times, and during the following 1800 years, the average expectancy of life was around forty years. Therefore we should read the story of Exodus, not as history, but as a spiritual interpretation of a lifetime's experience. If you are spiritually aware, you will find that during your lifetime you (like the Israelites in the wilderness) will need to take account of such matters as God/Law, God/Sin, God/Food and Drink, God/Health, God/Death, God/Promise. These are among the life-matters that are addressed by the writers and editors of the book Exodus. Also, and especially during Lent, we need to realise that Jesus, like ourselves, was tested (diabolically tempted) on and off throughout the whole of his lifetime, a fact distilled by the Gospel writers into the story of the forty days and nights in the wilderness. That is why Luke, at the end of his account, notes that the devil "departed from him *for a season*" (4.13).

In the light of all this, it would be no bad discipline for those of us who are over forty to find time each week (if not each day) during Lent to reflect and pray around the topic of *living on borrowed time*. We might include in our meditation the drastic imbalance between those who (in the so-called Western world) expect to survive intact into their nineties, and the millions of our fellow human beings in other parts of our planet who might consider themselves lucky if they ever reach their fortieth birthday.

# Giving it up
### Solihull Parish News February 2009

When it comes to reading the Bible, I certainly go along with Mark Twain who was once reputed to have said: "It's not the bits of the Bible that I _don't_ understand that give me trouble; it's the bits I _do_ understand that scare me." One of the scary bits is when Jesus says in Luke 14. 26, "Whoever comes to me and does not hate his father and mother, wife and children, brothers and sisters, yes even life itself, cannot be my disciple."

This is one of the occasions when Jesus is talking tough, exaggerating to drive home a point. When we come upon statements like this in his teaching, it is tempting to back off and find something more to our taste, like the Sermon on the Mount. But that won't do. We should be driven to engage with such sayings and try to understand just what Jesus was getting at.

First of all, it is quite important to realise that Jesus appears to have had a rocky relationship with his own family. At one stage they even thought that he was going out of his mind. Have a look at Mark 3.21, Mark 3. 31-35, Luke 8. 19-21, Matthew 12. 46-50, John 2.4. The author C.K. Stead in his novel about Jesus called _My Name was Judas_ exploits this, speculating that Jesus really did not get on with his mother and that the feeling was reciprocated. I am sure that this is not true. But there is no doubt that, in order to fulfil his ministry, Jesus did have to exercise detachment and practise renunciation. And those two words, _detachment_ and _renunciation_ are important when one is considering the meaning of true discipleship.

I would like to add to the list of sins, the sin of "clingy-ness" which shows itself in various kinds of ways. It could be an excessive dependence on a relative or friend which refuses to respect their freedom or their need sometimes to be alone. The classic instance of this is the over-possessive parent who can't let their child go. It could also simply be a compulsion to talk when the person you are talking to may be longing for you to be quiet. Or it might be acquisitiveness, and an excessive need to cling to possessions and a refusal to part with them. So in this harsh statement, Jesus is alerting us to the fact that, as Christian disciples, we must expect to adjust our priorities, consider carefully our relationships, and from time to time review what seemingly good things we may be called on to give up for the sake of Christ and the Gospel.

I am thinking about Bishop Hugh Montefiore. He was raised in a strict

Jewish family. When he was a teenager at Ruby School, he was literally called in a vision by Jesus to follow him. At that point, he hadn't even read the Gospels. He hadn't been allowed to. So he became a Christian, and his family were furious. Relationships were strained almost to breaking point, and for some of them it took years for reconciliation to happen. But Hugh virtually had no choice. He just knew that he had to become a disciple of Jesus, whatever the family might think or do.

I think also of a family that I knew years ago; I'll call them Smith. Mr Smith held a good job as the Midlands representative of a successful firm. As a consequence, he had a splendid home and all the trappings of affluence. Beginning as a nominal churchgoer, rather for appearances, he very quickly matured in the faith. As his discipleship deepened he became acutely aware that he could no longer reconcile the kind of selling that his company required him to do with his calling as a follower of Christ. Eventually he felt compelled to resign and seek other, less remunerative, employment. With a family of four school-age children, this was a hard choice to make. Fortunately Mrs Smith and the children stood by him, and they accepted a house move, and a considerable downsizing in their standard of living.

As Christians we may or may not have to face such stark decisions as Bishop Hugh and Mr Smith. But I think that those uncomfortable words of Jesus are there to remind us that our faith does include a principle of renunciation, and does require of us all a certain attitude of detachment. If God is truly our priority, then all other attachments, whether to people or to things, are of secondary importance. God has most certainly given us the good things of life to enjoy, but not to place our total reliance on. When you come to think of it, this is actually a very useful lesson that we are being asked to learn. To the degree that we take note of it, and put it into practise, we shall be that much better prepared for the time when all the good things of this life have inevitably to be set aside at its conclusion.

# Freedom and Challenge: God for Lent
## Solihull Parish News Lent 2011

On the threshold of the season of Lent, the Church asks us to consider the Transfiguration of Jesus. You will find the story in the ninth chapter of St Luke's Gospel. It tells of the time when three of those closest to Jesus went with him to the summit of Mount Tabor. There, during a time of intense prayer, Jesus suddenly shines with an inexpressibly glorious radiance. He seems to be accompanied by two figures from Jewish history, Moses and Elijah. A disembodied voice is heard. Jesus' companions, Peter, James and John, are totally confused: they experience mixed emotions, one of which is fear.

This is one of those moments when the veil between heaven and earth becomes very thin, almost transparent, and the glory of God shines through. It happened to the shepherds near Bethlehem, and they "were sore afraid." Momentarily, this heavenly glory puts the fear of God into those who experience it, and poses the big question, "What sort of God is this that we have to deal with?" I believe that question should be in our minds during the season of Lent and Easter.

To start you off, I want to suggest that our understanding of God is too narrow. In fact, the whole of the New Testament is written to make this point, and invites us to keep our idea of God constantly under review. Fear is one of the reactions that human beings have when God is taken seriously. This is not just a matter of being scared, like when you are in a nightmare. It is an attitude of wonder and respect and smallness in the face of something that is immense and awesome and powerful beyond imagining. We have a tendency to domesticate God, trying to bring him down to our level by confining him as far as possible inside a holy box called a church, and limiting his influence to about one day out of seven.

More dangerously still, we require God to be a God of love and compassion and forgiveness, exemplified by a Jesus who heals people, who blesses little children, and who tells interesting and odd stories. It is hardly surprising, then, that we tend to be completely thrown when we are faced with trying to make religious sense out of things like earthquakes and terminal illness. Perhaps people were better at this in the Middle Ages. That was a time when churches and cathedrals of staggering size and beauty were constructed: it was an age of great faith and scholarship and

Christian charity. At the same time the population was haunted by the Black Death and similar plagues, and most people were lucky to survive on this earth beyond the age of about thirty-five.

## Critique

Those Old Testament figures who appeared in the Transfiguration story, Moses and Elijah, were (as Jesus was) passionately concerned to get people to see that their conception of God was too small, limited and confined. Moses was the one who famously led the people from slavery to freedom, demonstrating the goodness of God who provides a promised land and will not fail or abandon his people. Let us also recall that Moses insisted on the rigorous discipline of the law and right behaviour.

Elijah was one of the prophets. They are not the kind of religious people who spend their time and energy pouring the fragrant oil of love and healing over the troubled waters of the human conscience. Their task and calling was to recall to our minds the holiness of God, and

to apply an incisive critique to the self-seeking behaviour of those in high places who ought to know better.

This was precisely the ministry that Jesus was about to embark on when he came down from Mount Tabor and made his way to Jerusalem. So he is depicted as the new Moses. Through the Cross, he will bring God's people to a new freedom from the endless cycle of sin and despair, even freedom from the tyranny and fear of death itself. Jesus is also the new Elijah, who will expose and challenge existing complacencies and life-styles.

It is these freedoms and challenges that must occupy our minds during the season of Lent, and help us to modify our attitudes and our behaviour, so that we may be more in line with the will of God according to the teaching of Jesus. At the same time, we shall do well to review and perhaps to modify our conception of God. I think there is a tendency that has appeared during the past hundred years for people to consider God as a parent whose job it is to spoil his human children and protect them from all possible harm. That is not the God of the Bible, the God and Father of our Lord Jesus Christ. The Biblical God would not score very highly on a modern 'health and safety' register. God certainly did not 'spoil' Jesus as an indulgent parent, nor will he spoil us. That means we have to contend with God who is as tough as he is tender, and who is as stern as he is loving. God cannot be known in his fullness nor manipulated in any way whatsoever. Consequently, we have to learn how to live with contradictions, including pain and suffering, problems for which we may find neither solutions nor logical reasons on this side of eternity.

Belief and trust in God is therefore as risky as it is comforting. In company with Jesus, however, it is infinitely worthwhile. In Jesus the glory of God shines through. In him we can understand afresh that the infinite, unknowable, and awesomely great God is enmeshed in his creation. However puzzling, or even tragic, events may seem from our perspective, all that happens has meaning and purpose.

We shall do well, during Lent, to remember that Scripture teaches us that "the fear of God is the beginning of wisdom". This fear may sometimes be a *frisson* of terror when we consider the immensity of God, but with connotations of awe, of respect, of obedience, and, of course, worship in its fullest sense.

**_St Mary and St John Lambton, Johannesburg_**

I was invited to do some teaching on contemplative prayer here and here-abouts in 2001. I arrived on a Friday in March. On Sunday the church held its Harvest Festival. Three days later it was Ash Wednesday, and I knew then for certain that I was in the Southern hemisphere. The sunny side of the nearby rectory where I was guest faced North, but the bath-water still vortexed down the plughole clockwise like at home (or was it anti-clockwise?).

My host pastored two other churches in addition to this one, one of which was situated in a Jo'burg township. The area looked to me like an English allotment on a vast scale: the sheds housed people.

I did this drawing sitting just inside the high steel security fence which surrounded the church and ancillary buildings. At the entrance gate stood the church notice board. "ST MARY AND ST JOHN. ALL ARE WELCOME" it proclaimed. Next to it was another notice which read: "CHUBB ALARMS: ARMED RESPONSE."

# CHAPTER THREE

# *Waiting Time*

## A Pregnant Pause
### Solihull Parish News November 2014

Some years ago I was asked to officiate at a funeral in a church not far from Solihull. The parish was in interregnum, and the undertakers had followed the usual practice of seeking help from retired clergy. The service was due to start at 9.30 a.m. I arrived at the church at about 8.45. The building appeared to be empty and all was quiet. As I was looking around to get my bearings, I became aware of a low murmuring sound. I made my way to the side chapel where it seemed to be coming from. There, rather to my surprise, I came across an elderly lady with a prayer book, sitting in a pew near the altar, quietly reciting a psalm. I stood in silence until she had finished, and then she became aware of my presence and turned to greet me.

"Sorry to interrupt," I said, "but I've come to take the funeral at half past nine." "Oh, yes," she replied, "I shall only be a few minutes. You see, when the last vicar was here, he used to say the office of Morning Prayer most days and I came sometimes. As we haven't got a vicar at the moment, I thought I would come each morning and say the prayers, at least until the new vicar arrives." We finished saying the office together and then she went home.

The psalm that she had been reciting was Psalm 40. Its Latin title in the Book of Common Prayer is evocative: *Expectans Expectavi* (I waited patiently). That seemed somehow very appropriate. Amidst all the busyness of a church managing without a vicar, and the inevitable tensions and anxieties of the process of finding and appointing a new priest, here was a humble soul undergirding everything with a faithful and persistent act of devotion.

Another point made itself felt at the time, giving a double sense of appropriateness, for the month was December, just at the start of the Advent season. I like to think of Advent as Simeon's season. Simeon was the old man who held the infant Jesus in the temple and spoke the Nunc

Dimittis (see Luke 2. 25-35). He is described by St. Luke as a devout person who had prayerfully "watched and waited" all his life for the coming of the Messiah-Saviour. Think again of Psalm 40: *I waited patiently for the Lord . . .*

*Expectans Expectavi.* In my younger days we weren't really supposed to say the word "pregnant", but we were allowed to say "expectant". I feel that this Latinate word does have a sort of light and joy, and an eager, forward-looking feel about it when a new baby is on the way. Using now the more earthy word, we might say that both Advent and a time of interregnum are a kind of pregnant pause. Following the Church's calendar, we do well to pause for a while with the expectant Mary, who is pregnant with the Word of God soon to become flesh to dwell among us. And in the time of interregnum, think of that lone parishioner who was faithfully praying the Daily Office as a kind of holy, and wholly essential, support for the ongoing work of the "church expectant."

◆

# Happy Christmas?
Mike's Musings Advent 2007

At the start of October, I decided to count how many times each day I heard the word "Christmas". After three days I lost count and gave up. The word used to be full of joy and expectation; now it is so debased in our society that it has become a word of dread. Like the word "holiday", which used to be "holy day", the sacred meaning of the word "Christmas" is submerged in the flood of consumerism, that engine of affluence, which drives human greed, selfishness, anxiety and stress.

What, as a Christian, can I do by way of protest? Very little, I fear; and that is partly because the Church itself is infected. The consumerist attitude is seen in the desperate desire for "success" measured simply by the size of congregations (I mean numerical size, of course). My only hope, I feel, is to use Advent profitably. This means, as far as I am able, dissociating myself from the persistent clamour of consumerism. This is far from easy. Jesus tells us not to be over-concerned with food and clothing – to "consider the birds of the air and the lilies of the field" and remember God's loving providence and care for creation. Yet I ask myself: "How much time do we spend at home thinking and talking about what we shall eat or what we shall wear?" The answer is: "an awful lot".

Advent is supposed to be a fast, like Lent. These four weeks should be a time to make a renewed effort to exercise Christian discipline and self-control. Advent is given as an opportunity to try harder to focus on things that really matter: love, peace, sin and judgment, life, death and the here-after – in other words, "God's kingdom" in which consumerism literally has no place because it is nothing more than a deadly delusion.

I am not an ascetic; one cursory glance at my waistline will indicate that. But during Advent I shall once again try to undertake a small act of self-denial, and attempt to polish up my daily commitment to prayer and bible reading. And I shall try to operate my selective hearing in order to become a little more deaf to the advertisers' noise, and a little more aware of the voice of God within.

And in my letter-writing (which is quite considerable) I shall not wish my correspondents "Happy Christmas" because the word is debased and the festival has been hijacked by our consumerist society, and I have serious doubts that it is possible to have a happy Christmas in the context now provided by manufacturers and advertisers. Instead, I shall conclude my letters, "Wishing you a blessed Nativity-tide" or something similar. Such a choice of words focuses on the truth behind the festival of Christ's birth, which begins, not on October 1$^{st}$, but at Evensong on December 24$^{th}$, and continues through to Epiphany on January 6$^{th}$ or to Candlemas on February 2$^{nd}$.

—◦—

# Wartime Christmas
### Solihull Parish News December 2015

Inevitably as each Christmas comes round, I look back to my childhood, and experience that magical afterglow of memory when so much of what has happened between then and now has been forgotten. My grand-mother, whom I never knew (she died before I was born), was half German. Consequently in my mother's childhood home, conversation was bilingual. And so, in a sense, was their celebration of Christmas, with a bias towards customs that my grandmother had brought from Germany. This legacy was passed on to the next generation.

Early last December, during the first week of Advent, an acquaintance of mine was hanging trimmings on the artificial Christmas tree that he had just bought. "I'm not sure when I should be decorating this", he declared as he fixed a bauble. I responded firmly, "It should properly be done on Christmas Eve, not before." He looked at me in total disbelief. At my home when I was a child, we began to make paper chains about a week before Christmas. They were contrived out of strips of coloured paper, the links stuck together with flour-and-water paste. This was wartime: austerity prevailed. But we didn't hang the chains up until Christmas Eve.

The memory is strong. I come from a large family. On Christmas Eve It is the privilege of the older children to decorate the Christmas tree. We younger ones are debarred from the sitting room while this is going on, but we know with mounting excitement that our presents are also being arranged in discreet personal locations round the room. They will not be under the tree: that space is reserved for the lovely old German crib figures which Mother had inherited from her family.

After what seems like an eternity of waiting, we are finally summoned after tea to assemble outside the sitting room door. The lights are turned off. We hold our breath, trying to control our nervous tension. There may be memories of what is about to happen, but for a young child, Christmases are so far apart that every one is the first time. The door opens. We go in. And there is the tree, which we last saw bare, shedding needles as it was carried into the house. Now we behold it in all its splendour, lit with real candles clipped to its branches, glorious with the sparkling fragility of the German glass ornaments which had survived from my Mother's own childhood.

Then – presents? No, not yet. First we honour the Christ child in the crib by singing a few carols, with Mary and Joseph, the shepherds, the kings and the animals, kneeling or standing close by. Then at last we are shown to our individual little piles of gifts. And all this happens on Christmas Eve, so that on Christmas Day we are free to go as a family to the Morning Service in church.

These memories stem from a wartime childhood. In spite of the austerity and sombre background, I still reckon that I was privileged. By Christmas 1945, the war was over, but there were still some German prisoners-of-war in England waiting repatriation. We gave hospitality to one of them. Lucky fellow! Mother of course was able to converse fluently with him in his own language, and for his brief stay he became one of the family. We were in the throes of preparing for our Nativity tableaux in church. Hans declared how much he enjoyed helping us to make "flies for the engel", i.e. Gabriel's wings! It was very moving to see his response to our customary Christmas routine, which of course was an echo of his own childhood experience back home.

So: has the modern commercial Christmas 'hype' obliterated all traces of the real thing? Do I just have to rely on nostalgic memories in order to recapture something authentic from the past? Perhaps it is so. But let's not forget that Jesus advised us to "become like little children." If we take note of that, I think we can rescue the great message of the arrival of the world's Saviour from the seasonal litter of hollow advertising and bank notes. The mystery and the magic are still there at the heart of it when we remember to reach out in love to Him whose birthday we are celebrating. At the same time, in our dealings with others, let us continually try, and especially at Christmas time (as Gilbert Shaw so eloquently put it) "to put love in where love is not."

**Driffield, East Yorkshire**

I love canals. Living in the middle of England as I do, as far from the sea as you can get in any direction, these quiet waterways compensate for the fact that I miss the watery coastline where I spent most of my youthful years.

Birmingham reputedly has more canals than Venice. They may not have quite the same allure, but we should be proud that, unlike their pretty Italian counterparts, Birmingham's canals were constructed 800 feet above sea level. The appropriate technology to achieve this is graphically illustrated by a signpost in Worcester. It is situated by the first lock where the southward canal from Birmingham joins the river Severn. One finger reads, *Gloucester 25 miles: 1 lock*. The other, *Birmingham 30 miles: 58 locks*.

Who knows? As our motorways become increasingly clogged up with slow-moving traffic, commercial carriers may find that a barge pulled along by a plodding horse might achieve the same average speed as a lorry. Then our inland waterways might become the arterial roads of the future as they were in the past.

The sketch above was done in my home county of Yorkshire, not least because of the industrial archaeology which I also take much pleasure in. I was quite pleased with it: it looks as though the crane might actually work, not collapse as some of my other drawings of old machines appear to indicate.

CHAPTER FOUR

# Time and Eternity

## The Time Capsule

Solihull Parish News July/August 2016

The parish church of St Mary Magdalene in Tanworth-in-Arden was sensibly and sensitively restored by the Victorians during the 1880s, with generous support from a benefactor who was living at the time in Henley-in-Arden. During the 1980s, we decided to celebrate the centenary of this happy restoration with a Victorian weekend, a flower festival and various other frolicsome events in and around the village.

The children of the church school were naturally involved. Children in church today are often referred to as "The Church of tomorrow". That description is not entirely apt, for all who are baptised are members of the Church *now*, irrespective of age. Nevertheless, it is right for us sometimes to reflect on tomorrow's Church. And at a time of centenary celebration, we felt it would not be amiss to think of the Church in one hundred years' time. In the year 2083, what will they think of us?

So the top class of the school prepared a time capsule for their successors. As you might expect, a lot of discussion took place about what it should contain, for space was very limited. Eventually, the children compiled their list. Among the objects was a television licence, a postage stamp, a glass marble, a 45 r.p.m. pop record, and some photos of the children themselves. These, together with a number of other small items were selected as objects that would speak of today to the children of tomorrow. Each was painstakingly wrapped and protected against the ravages of time, then carefully placed into a biscuit tin.

On the following Sunday morning, the tin itself, meticulously over-wrapped and sealed, was brought to church. There it became a focal point for an all-age family service, which had the theme "Time". We were able to reflect on the past, the 600-year-old building in which we were worshipping, so lovingly preserved and cared for over the centuries. We thought of the church that it had replaced, reaching even further back in time. We considered our own experience of time, in particular its elasticity: how it races by for the elderly and so often dawdles for the young when they are waiting for Christmas: how it disappears altogether when we are asleep, and how it stretches out into unimaginable figures in the realm of space.

## The unborn

Now came the fulcrum of the service, which tipped us from the past to the future. At the back of the church there is an ancient piece of furniture that actually pre-dates the present building by about 200 years. It is a massive parish chest, hewn out of the solid trunk of a single oak tree from the surrounding forest of Arden. It is interesting that it is not only this chest, now black with age and hard as iron, that has survived the centuries, but also the word "trunk" to describe a storage facility. A local carpenter had prepared a kind of box inside the chest located at one end. Half way through the service, we carried our time capsule to the back of the church and solemnly placed it in its own compartment. Here it was screwed down and a notice on the lid explained what it was, and indicated the date in the 2080s when it should be opened.

During the time of prayer that followed, we did something quite unusual and thought-provoking: we prayed for the unborn, and in particular for those who, in a hundred years time, would open our time capsule. I am sure that many of us will have prayed in the past for our children and those of our relatives and friends while they were still in the womb. On one occasion, I administered the laying-on-of-hands on, or, rather, through the rounded belly of a member of my congregation. The expectant mother had had great difficulty in bringing a child to birth and asked for special prayers. To our relief and joy, the boy was born, and became a strong and healthy child. In addition to baptising him, I was asked to be his godfather. I am pleased to say that he remains strong and healthy in middle age.

Have we ever included in our intercessions those who will be born twenty, fifty, or a hundred years hence? Probably not, and we should not berate ourselves on that account. For the idea takes us beyond the edge of our imagining and into the more mystical realms of religious experience and understanding. The prophet Jeremiah caught a momentary glimpse of this scope of God's love when he heard God say to him: *Before I formed you in the womb I knew you* (1.5). God's love and knowledge of his creation, especially his human creation, is both timeless and boundless.

Here, then, is the specially composed Prayer for the Unborn which we used in our centenary service to balance our thanksgiving for the rich heritage of the Church's past:

*Almighty God, our heavenly Father,*
*all-knowing, all-wise, all-loving,*
*to you belong all the ages of humankind,*
*as you dwell beyond all space and time*
*in the glory of eternity.*

*Hear our prayers today*
*for your children yet unborn*
*(especially for those who, living in a new age,*
*will bring to light in a hundred years' time*
*the simple objects that we have prepared for them).*

*We pray that they, like us,*
*may know the consolation of your love.*
*May we and they together*
*grow in grace as we share your glory,*
*the glory that is revealed for us throughout all ages*
*in him in whose Name we pray,*
*even Jesus Christ, your Son, our Lord. Amen*

# Time and Eternity (1)

*This is the first of two related articles.*

Solihull Parish News January 2011

Normally, if I start to read a book and then realise that I cannot understand it, I put it down again and start another. That seems like common sense. Recently I deviated from common sense, began to read a book, was able to understand almost none of it, and read it from cover to cover. That book was called *A Brief History of Time* by Stephen Hawking.

The author has become a household name and something of a celebrity. He is known as someone who, in spite of being severely disabled and confined to a wheelchair with motor neurone disease, has become the world's most brilliant theoretical physicist since Einstein. His book, first published in 1988 and reprinted many times, is supposedly written for the non-mathematical layman (that describes me pretty accurately!). It surveys briefly the world's great theories of the cosmos from Aristotle to Einstein. It also indicates the author's great concern to search for a Grand Unified Theory that will explain everything-that-is in terms of general relativity and quantum mechanics.

I suppose I finished the book because I was mesmerised both by the language and the concepts, even though I was largely unclear about the meaning. Hawking's thinking is "out of this world" as we experience it. He is dealing with the impossibly large and the infinitely minuscule. He uses mind-blowing numbers and unimaginable distances and aeons of time. He speaks of galaxies and universes, electrons and protons, and neutrons. Quantities are given, not just in millions, but in millions of millions, e.g. "the number 1 with 80 zeros after it." A glance through the Glossary and Index shows us some of the arcane vocabulary used to express this kind of theorising: not just words that we have become familiar with like *atoms* and *electrons*, but *neutrons* and *neutrinos*, *quarks* and *quanta*, *gravitons*, *positrons* and *pulsars*, *antiparticles* and *singularities*.

We are perhaps familiar with the theory of the "big bang" which kick-started our universe, perhaps also with the "big crunch" with which it is assumed that it will end after collapsing in on itself. I find myself entering very mysterious territory when asked to consider "virtual particles", "imaginary time", and statements such as: "The boundary condition of the universe is that it has no boundary".

I expected that the word "God" would appear sooner or later, and I was not disappointed. Hawking mentions God several times, usually fairly casually as a possible cause of creation, or as a possible reason for the universe being as it is (or as it appears to be from the scientist's point of view). Einstein believed in God, and once asked the rhetorical question, "How much choice did God have in constructing the universe?" Hawking's attitude is very much like that of the early 19th century scientist Laplace. When he was asked how God fitted in to his scientific view of creation he replied, "I have no need of that hypothesis."

**Unified**

Stephen Hawking is looking for a complete unified scientific and mathematical theory of everything and he seems to think that, one day, human beings will discover one. He avoids the arrogant atheism of Richard Dawkins and he is sufficiently humble to allow his clever book to end with unanswered questions: "Why does the universe go to all the bother of existing?", and, "Is the unified theory so compelling that it brings about its own existence? Or does it need a creator, and, if so, does he have any other effect on the universe? And who created him?"

However, in spite of the book's title, the mystery of time and eternity remains unresolved, and I am personally not helped by being required to consider "infinities" in the plural, "imaginary numbers", "imaginary time", or, that space-time "on a very small scale is ten-dimensional."

I will admit that I read the book because, at my stage in life, time has become rather important. Where scientists and mathematicians struggle to express themselves, the spiritual tradition achieves better clarity. In my next article I want to say something about God and time. I find that I cannot raise much enthusiasm about a cosmic beginning that happened thousands of millions of years ago, or a cosmic crunch that might occur thousands of millions of years in the future. Just now, I find it difficult to call to mind what happened last week! But a God who exists outside time, yet created time for our good – that, I think, is an absorbing and important subject. These words from the third chapter of Ecclesiastes in the Old Testament will serve as a kind of bridge between this article and the next. After the well-known passage about there being a time for everything, "a time to be born and a time to die, a time to plant and time to uproot" etc. the writer says in verse 11, "God has made everything to suit its time; moreover he has given mankind a sense of past and future, but no comprehension of God's work from beginning to end."

# Time and Eternity (2)
## Solihull Parish News February 2011

I ended my first article about time with a quotation from Ecclesiastes 3.11 (see above). In his book *A Brief History of Time*, Stephen Hawking refers to his quest for a complete theory of everything. In pursuit of this quest, he brings together a phenomenal mathematical intellect and the remarkable discoveries of modern science in the realms of cosmology and particle physics. At the end of his book, the author looks forward to the possibility that, eventually, with more research, human beings could arrive at such a theory: "Then we shall all, philosophers, scientists, and just ordinary people, be able to take part in the discussion of the question of why it is that we and the universe exist. If we find the answer to that, it would be the ultimate triumph of human reason – for then we would know the mind of God."

At that point, Hawking very wisely leaves the question open and his discourse ends. Those of us who, in faith, follow a spiritual path may now take it on from there. First of all, we come to terms with the fact that, in this physical universe, we live in a time framework. As part of the scientifically educated modern Western culture, we tend to lay great emphasis on the measurement and passing of time. Against this, we need to remember that the **spiritual** realm, which, as God's children, we also inhabit, lies totally outside time. So in the Bible, God, who is able to declare himself as "I AM" (in the present tense) announces through St John, "I AM the Alpha and the Omega, who is and who was and who is to come" (Revelation 1.8), "The first and the last" (1.17. See also Isaiah 41.4 & 44.6). God is therefore the One who dwells in the eternal present. To this, God adds the rhetorical question, "Do I not fill heaven (the spiritual realm) and earth (the realm of physical creation)?" So God is quite literally Lord of all, a lordship that in Christian theology, God shares with the Son (Christ) and the Holy Spirit.


**God moments**

We view time as an ordered system of years, days, hours, minutes and seconds, but our experience tells us that time is in fact remarkably fluid. I remember myself as a child, waiting for Christmas, and how time dragged its feet. Now the days and even the years flip by at an extraordinary speed. What happened to time when we were babies? What happens to it when we are asleep? When I was young, I had no time for girls, until I fell in love: then it was remarkable how much time I discovered!

In attempting to grasp this idea of God in the eternal present, I find Alan Watts a useful guide. I quote from his book "Behold the Spirit" (Vintage Books 1972):

*The focal point of Reality is now – this present moment, this elusive image of eternity, so small that it has no temporal length and yet so long that we can never escape from it. Here in this present moment life is most lively; here alone do we really exist. The past is dead; the future as yet is not…This moment is our life, but the more we try to hold it, the faster it slips away. We look for it and cannot find it because it is too small to see, too slippery to hold, and yet this is where we are given union with God … However hard we may fight to retain the past or to hurry on into the future, we cannot get out of the present moment. The more we try to hold it, the more we fail to perceive that it holds us. The moment always carries us in its embrace … To understand this is simplicity itself.*

*And here is the perfect analogy of our union with God – a reality which possesses and holds us as surely and as presently as the moment, a reality which in some sense is this moment … What we have to realise, therefore, is not the getting of union with God, but the not being able to get away from it. It is in, it is this Eternal Now, wherein God so lovingly holds us.*

In the light of this, I am beginning tentatively to experience in my prayer-life what I call "God moments." These are moments, probably lasting less than a minute, possibly only a few seconds, when the reality of God is all that matters. Each "moment" begins with a clear understanding that neither I nor anyone else, nor anything in creation, has existed in the future.[6] This means that the next few seconds, or minutes, in which I am about to exist, are completely untouched virgin territory, containing only God and known only to him. So I am about to enter a real and totally overwhelming experience of eternity – an explorer taking the very first step on a new, unknown and empty continent.

---

6   Stephen Hawking would probably not agree with this, for in his topsy-turvy universe which somehow curves in on itself, time could conceivably go backward [see pages 148-150 in his book]

The "God moment" that I experience is awesome and could be, fleetingly, a moment of terror as much as of joy or fulfilment. This is because, at such a moment, you can be briefly aware of void and emptiness, being on the brink of the unknown and the unknowable, as well as aware of the infinite power of God. Before this timeless "moment" itself happens, I may briefly call to mind the remarkable universe revealed to scientists and mathematicians such as Stephen Hawking, with its literally countless millions of stars and universes, its vast distances measured in light-years, its ungraspable numbers of sub-atomic particles. Equally, the "moment" may be prompted by some great pain or tragedy, actual or remembered, or a truly joyful recollection, or perhaps a deep desire to be sorry, or to be thankful. Such thoughts or feelings may go with me into the "moment" but are not the focus of it. For the focus is *only* God-in-eternity, the everlasting I AM in the eternal present.

It is difficult, as always, to find words adequately to express just what is happening when one is at the edge of deep mystery. I know it as a "God moment", and I believe that it is to do with the union with God that Alan Watts writes about. It is connected with prayer, but it is neither prayer nor worship, nor indeed is it meditation or even contemplation. These things continue alongside, to help us to develop our spiritual potential. The "God moment", however, is very brief, but very real. It is a moment of "time out". As Alan Watts says: "It is **_in_**, it **_is_**, this Eternal Now, wherein God so lovingly holds us."

***Archangel Michael Chapel, Lefkara, Cyprus***

A trip abroad to a popular holiday and wedding destination, not that I personally go there often, i.e. once in a lifetime, but it was for a wedding and a holiday. Both were fascinating. My niece Liz was not married in this church, but in the courtyard of a town museum. There the ceremony was conducted, very nicely I thought, by the town mayor, who was happy for me to add a Christian (C of E) blessing. Glancing through a window behind where the mayor was standing, I noticed one of the museum's exhibits: a large iron double bed with brass knobs, beside which was an old-style child's cot draped in white muslin. I thought the mayor had chosen his location well.

The Byzantine church of St Michael amazingly takes one back a thousand years. It seems not to have altered much during the whole millennium. We found it more or less by chance, rather tucked away off the general tourist route. I'm glad we did, not only for sketching purposes, but because of the remarkably well-preserved medieval frescoes on the walls.

Talking of weddings, when I attended Anglican worship the following Sunday in Ayia Napa, the English chaplain there told me that he now needed secretarial help with the increase in matrimonial paperwork. When he took over the job three years before, he officiated during his first year at just three weddings for couples from England. This current year the number had risen to well over a hundred. I believe that the Isle of Cyprus has some connection with Venus. Ask the travel agents!

# CHAPTER FIVE

# Ministry and Ministers

## A New Ministry
### Solihull Parish News September 2015

In Matthew 21.23 and the subsequent verses, we read how Jesus was challenged by "the priests and elders of the nation" as he was teaching in the temple. "By what authority (they said) are you acting like this?" That was a burning question for the established religious hierarchy of Jerusalem. They were faced with a Galilean ex-carpenter who had become a popular, successful, charismatic and critical upstart religious leader. In response to their challenge, Jesus exercises his sovereign freedom under God, and simply turns the question back on to his challengers, calling John the Baptist as witness.

When a church and parish is poised at the start of a new ministry, the appointed minister comes with authority. Their authority will not be the same as that of Jesus, but it is a reflection of it, and derives from it. The Church of England, in its structures, is sensitive to this question of divine authority. When a new priest is licensed or instituted, the bishop reiterates the statement that "The Church of England is part of the One Holy Catholic and Apostolic Church ..." Those people who have been truly called by God to exercise the priestly ministry in the Church are invested with the divine authority to fulfil their calling. At their ordination, the bishop says: "Take (thou) authority ..." to preach, teach, and administer the sacraments. This is a delegated authority from God, mediated by the Holy Spirit through the Body of Christ, the Holy Catholic Church. The local ministry, therefore, bears resemblance to the ministry of Jesus. It also shares to some extent that sovereign freedom that Jesus demonstrated.

The historical structure of our Church means that the minister exercises his responsibility towards a congregation, the gathered people of God, and with their cooperation, towards the parish which, in the case of the Church of England, is a geographical area. We are *not* a congregational Church. Occasionally, you hear about a parish, deprived for some reason of a vicar, saying, "Why can't we just find our own person, and pay him or her?" Or, in a more sinister vein, a parish church which holds to a partisan doctrine may be at odds with the bishop and try to "go it alone" and appoint their own minister to fit the dogma.

Such independent initiatives, apart from disrupting the Body of Christ, will inevitably actually deprive the minister of that sovereign freedom which is an essential part of the ministry. To put it baldly, if a congregation pays the vicar, then that congregation will expect to hear from the vicar what it *wants* to hear, which may well be not at all what it *ought* to be hearing.

**Relationship**
The Church of England structures and its parish system have a great deal to commend them in this respect. The relationship between a parish priest and the lay church members is subtle and sometimes precarious. On the one hand, the congregation must recognise and honour the authority of the minister, together with the sovereign freedom which his authority implies. At the same time, the clergy, also recognising their intrinsic authority and freedom, have to accept the pastoral responsibility of exercising that spiritual privilege with tact as well as firmness, with discretion as well as courage. In all this, the minister's focus must always remain on the pole star of Christ – the truths of his Gospel and the love in his heart.

These are exciting and challenging times for the Church. There may well be great changes to be faced, both locally and on a broader front. At such times, it is important to keep a firm grasp on the essentials of the faith, as well as recognising and valuing those Church structures by which the faith is maintained and propagated in the local community.

———————◄◦►———————

# The Alphabet of Ministry
Solihull Parish News December 2006

*(Note. In the following article, please excuse the use of the masculine pronoun referring to priests. This is not intended to express a point of view regarding women priests; it is simply to avoid a certain clumsiness in style by a repetitious use of "he/she" in the text.)*

There is no career structure in the sacred ministry of the Church. That may come as a surprise to many people, including some clergy. But the fact is, that once a person has been ordained as a priest, they have reached the pinnacle, spiritually speaking, of the ministry. They may have the ability to take on weightier responsibilities within the structure of the Church, but even a bishop would agree that what really counts is his priesthood.

So what is a priest really for? What are priests ordained to do? I can hear a welter of answers coming from churchgoers and others … visiting, preaching and teaching, chairing committees, attracting people to church, public relations, dealing with christenings and weddings and funerals, leading and managing, praying and presiding at church services, studying books. Certainly, priests will be found carrying out such tasks as these. But then, when you come to think of it, so are lots of other people. It is important to ask again, what is actually distinctive about the priesthood, which marks this ordained status off from other jobs or callings?

My answer is a lesson I learnt long ago, when I was training for the ministry – a simple and basic memory-aid called "The ABC of the Priesthood". **A** for Absolution. **B** for Benediction. **C** for Consecration.

**A**bsolution … the forgiving of sins
**B**enediction … the invoking and imparting of God's blessing
**C**onsecration … the setting apart of bread and wine for sacred use in the Holy Communion.

In our Anglican Church tradition, which reaches back into the early years of Christianity, these are three spiritual functions that have been formally reserved for the ordained priest. At the service of ordination, the bishop, representing the whole Church, gives authority to those who are called to be priests specifically to carry out these functions.

**A** for Absolution

The priest, and no one else, formally pronounces God's forgiveness to penitent sinners. He may do this in a public service following the prayer of Confession, usually, but not always, making the sign of the cross. Or he may do it in private, when an individual makes a confession of sin in his hearing. The priest's authority to do this is clearly set out in the 1662 Book of Common Prayer in the service for the Visitation of the Sick.

**B** for Benediction

The priest, and no one else, is also authorised to give a formal blessing. The most familiar form of this is at the end of a service of worship. The

Church recognises the priest as one who is set apart to be, in a sense, God's representative. In this capacity, he is empowered (like Aaron in the Old Testament) to "put God's Name" on the people … which is what Benediction actually means. In this way, the priest acts as a channel for the flowing out of God's goodness for the benefit of His creation, specifically for His human creation.

C for Consecration

The third function of the Christian priesthood is to celebrate the Holy Communion. This involves the setting-apart, or consecration, of the bread and wine. This food and drink is then received by the priest and the faithful laity as the sacramental life of Christ, body and blood, spiritual nourishment for the Christian journey through life. Once again, it is our Church tradition that only the ordained priest may do this. That in itself marks this service of Eucharist as special. It is a deeply symbolic act of worship in which the consecrating priest, representing both God and God's people, stands close to the mystery of sacrifice like the Old Testament priests. Only now, of course, he is relating spiritually to the sacrifice of Jesus on the Cross.

That, then, is what a priest is for: Absolution, Benediction, and Consecration. That is his function. That is what priests are ordained for. And those three tasks must remain as the focus of any priestly ministry. But this *sacred* ministry does not and cannot operate in a vacuum. There must be a context for it. And the context is the congregation, the gathered community, called by God to follow the way of Christ in living and in worship. And this Christ-community is itself set in the wider context of the world, however you may wish to define "the world". Consequently, those three functions of the priesthood are shared with the congregation. They actually find their true significance in the lives of every member. And here we find ourselves at the cutting edge of the Gospel.

In terms of **Absolution**

It is often said these days that we live in a culture of blame. There is a prevailing atmosphere of punishment, revenge and retaliation. It is not only in the Middle East. You only have to look at the headlines in the popular press in our own country. Against this, the Gospel sets *forgiveness*. This is not simply an alternative to revenge. It is a prime necessity. Forgiveness is embedded in the fabric of authentic Christianity, and it is at the centre of our own banner-headline prayer: "Forgive us … as we forgive …." The priestly ministry of Absolution must relate to this wider aspect of forgiveness, not only in our attitude to the world, but in our dealings with each other.

## In terms of **Blessing**

A formal blessing from a priest may engender within us a good feeling and a sense that God's goodness prevails. I see nothing wrong in that. But let us translate this function of blessing into day-to-day living. What are the *blessings* of modern life? There are many. But these are confusing times, and we need to try to think clearly and evaluate the nature of some blessings that we might take for granted, and ask, "are they truly Godly?" How Godly, for example, are the blessings of modern technology? Good health is a blessing. But do we ever ask what the blessing of good health is for? These are searching questions, and they carry assumptions that Christians need to be challenging, especially about our use or mis-use of natural and financial resources.

## In terms of **Consecration**

This function also has a corporate nature about it. Only a priest can perform this sacred duty, but he cannot do it on his own. The rules of the Church state that someone else must be present at Holy Communion for the service to be valid. There are many aspects to the profound significance of this sharing in Holy Communion. However, a key element, as the words "consecration" and "sacrament" imply, is the *sacrality* of the action. This is not just a fellowship meal. When the offered bread is broken and the wine is blessed, when the priest re-presents the Lord Jesus at His Supper, when he speaks the remembered words "This is my body… this is my blood…" both priest and people are entering deeply into the mystery of sacrifice, the mysteries of pain and suffering, as well as of death and resurrection, and of hope and promise and joy. The bread and wine become *sacred*, set apart for holy purpose. And all of us who receive it are ourselves then also set apart to become, in a sense, priests to the world.

Our Western world in general has lost the sense of the sacred. Once that happens and nothing is sacred, then the world becomes simply a collection of physical objects to be exploited, and its inhabitants, soul-less and secular, become little more than biological units to be manipulated by powerful and clever people. Christians cannot and must not go down that path, for we are in touch with the Divine, with the mystery of Christ. We are called, set apart, to assert and proclaim the *sacred-ness* of God's creation, and to discern, recognise and carry out the loving purposes of God within it. In that sense, we all share in the consecration at Holy Communion, and we are ourselves consecrated – sacred fragments in a spiritual cosmos, and as such we are precious in the sight of God.

In a complex and often confusing world, it is important to remember that our priests are called and ordained to Absolve, to Bless and to Consecrate. At the same time, as Christians, we should continually be working out how we personally fit into these key functions … our own spiritual alphabet of forgiveness, blessing, and leading a consecrated life as part of the priesthood of Christ.

# The Sacred Ministry
Solihull Parish News November 2004

There are four times during the Church's year when, by tradition, ordinations take place – during Advent, during Lent, around St Peter's Day (June) and around Michaelmas (September). At these times, three days during one week are designated as Ember Days[7] when we are bidden to pray for those to be ordained.

At ordination, a person is commissioned to a sacred function. He or she, having assured the Church that they have been called by God, is set apart, selected carefully from the Christian body, and given a mandate to serve in that body as a leader with authority to carry out specific tasks. Those tasks, or duties, may be divided into two broad categories. One is the task of prayer and worship. This is to do with personal spiritual development, and also with the leading of public worship – church services of one kind or another. The other task is to engage with the Christian community in some specific location, and, through that community, to

---

[7]   The word 'ember' in this context has nothing to do with ashes. It merely means 'season', or more accurately a regularly recurring season (from the Old English *ymb-ryne*, literally *running around*, i.e. a circuit of times and seasons in the course of the year).

engage also with the wider society who may or may not share the Christian faith. This engagement will involve, among other things, teaching, evangelism, and pastoral care.

In the Church of England (and other Anglican churches), ordination will make a man or woman a deacon or a priest. In a few special cases it will make a person a bishop, but that process is more commonly called "consecration" and, for practical purposes in this article, we can set it aside. Ordination will not make a person a vicar, or a rector, or a curate, or a chaplain, or a reverend. These are merely labels to indicate tasks or status.

Nor, it should be said, will ordination make a person into a saint ... i.e. after ordination a person will not automatically become morally perfect and capable of leading an unblemished life. In that respect, the ordained man or woman never ceases to share in the struggle towards holiness with the rest of the Christian community. It is fair that the community should expect from their clergy high standards and, as far as possible, exemplary conduct. It is **not** fair that they should expect fault-free or perfect behaviour.

## Structures

It is interesting that neither Jesus nor his followers in the first century left any very clear picture of how the Christian Church and religion should be organised, or how the Church should conduct its affairs. The Lord himself left no written records, and the early Christian writings are confused on questions of organisation and structure. Indeed, it is by no means certain that Jesus ever intended to found a new religion, and it is doubtful whether many of his first century followers would have wanted to do so.

Gradually, however, as the novelty and impact of the Gospel began to make their mark, the Christian movement became organised and the Church began to take shape; or perhaps one should say "began to take shapes" in the plural. Because whatever the Roman Catholic and Orthodox Churches may think or teach, at no time has there ever been a single unified and monolithic Church structure embracing all Christians.

Some people would argue that Christianity and organisation are not compatible. They look at the Gospel, at the poverty and the simplicity of the lifestyle of Jesus and his companions, and they find it difficult to reconcile this with the elaborate structures and liturgies and buildings that the

Christian Churches have produced during twenty centuries. The apparent mismatch of Gospel and Church was amusingly summed up some years ago in a lecture given by a former Dean of Windsor. He was reflecting on the contrast between Jesus, the carpenter-turned-itinerant-preacher from Nazareth, and himself as one who was caught up amid the splendours and ceremonies of the Royal Chapel. "Sometimes (he said), as I sit in my rather plush surroundings to exercise my Christian ministerial duties, I cannot help thinking that, whereas, as Saint Luke puts it, the Son of Man had nowhere to lay his head, the Dean of Windsor puts his bum on a velvet cushion."

The contrast is indeed stark, and the point is made effectively, and raises some interesting and challenging questions about the nature of the Gospel, and that of the Church and its structuring. The Gospel is, of course, provocative; but it is also glorious and joyful. At the same time it is mediated among real people in human societies, and such societies themselves depend on structures and organisation. It is not surprising, therefore, that Christian groupings, Churches, which exist to proclaim the glory and the joy of the Gospel and to serve and to challenge society, must themselves be effectively organised and structured if they are to carry out their sacred tasks in the real world.

**Sacredness**

The ordained ministry is an integral part of that structuring. The ministers may, on occasion, be part of pomp and ceremonies which are arranged principally to reflect on earth something of the heavenly glory. Occasionally, therefore, they may place their posteriors on velvet cushions. But let us not forget that their calling and their tasks are sacred. In the world of today, the concept of sacredness is barely understood. The Church's sacred ministers are consequently more likely to be found sticking their necks out, or placing their heads on blocks, in a variety of vulnerable and stressful positions. For this is so often the destiny of those who dare to speak of God's justice, of the forgiving compassion of Christ, and of the virtues of self-denial and restraint, when so many are hell-bent on self-satisfaction, short-term gains, and personal comfort and gratification at other people's expense.

Finally, it should be remembered that sacred ministers depend on sacred congregations. A priest is not primarily looking for individuals or groups who are dedicated to fetes, brilliant with Brownies, or splendid at social activities, however useful or enjoyable such things may be. The ordained minister will best serve, and be served by, a congregation who love their Lord, who are striving for beauty in worship and for holiness in life, who long for heaven, and who will shine with the joy of the Gospel.

In this connection, one of the traditional Good Friday collects is apt and relevant both for sacred ministers and sacred congregations:

*Almighty and everlasting God, by whose Spirit the whole body of the Church is governed and sanctified; hear our prayer which we offer for all your faithful people; that each in his or her vocation and ministry may serve you in holiness and truth to the glory of your Name: through our Lord and Saviour Jesus Christ. Amen.*

***Clifford's Tower, York***

I chickened out, and sketched this instead of York Minster! Why is it called Clifford's Tower? Nobody seems to know. The name first appears around 1600 when there were people of that name in the city. But other sources link it with other Cliffords who lived much earlier. A fortification was built here by William the Conqueror shortly after 1066. Nothing remains of that, and this tower was built during the 13th century.

My most memorable visit to York happened in 2010. I was accorded the privilege of officiating at a service of Holy Communion in the Minster one hundred years after my father was ordained there by Archbishop Cosmo Gordon Lang in 1910. The usual Saturday midday congregation was augmented by a merry influx of about fifty of my close relatives and friends.

After the service we gathered for a family meal in the atmospheric medieval surroundings of Saint William's College close by the Minster. I was a touch late for lunch because I got locked in the vestry by mistake. It was some time before I was able to make my escape, clutching the two decorated cast-iron door handles that I had pulled off in my efforts to force the double doors. I handed them over with apologies to an official who looked at me rather quizzically.

So perhaps Clifford's Tower is not so out of place after all, seeing that the site and its buildings have frequently been used as a prison during the past 900 years.

# CHAPTER SIX

# *Jerusalem*

## Jerusalem the Golden
### Mikes Musings September 2006

To visit Jerusalem as a pilgrim is an unforgettable experience. For the ordinary tourist it is pretty stunning: for a pilgrim it is mind-blowing. It bears, of course, no resemblance to the city that Jesus knew. Yet simply to pace the present-day streets and visit the places that hold the memories of past centuries, and to worship there, where Jesus taught, and stayed and died and rose again, that, in itself, is an overwhelming spiritual privilege. Once you have done that, life is never quite the same again.

I was looking at an old map of the world recently. Most of it consisted of what we would recognise as the old Roman Empire. Beyond that, around the edges, it got a bit vague and bizarre. Interestingly, almost at the centre of it was Jerusalem. That was quite deliberate on the part of the mapmaker, because within Christendom, as in Judaism, Jerusalem is the mystic centre of the earth.

Towards the end of the Bible, in the 21$^{st}$ chapter of the book *Revelation*, there is a passage which includes St John's vision of the New Jerusalem. This is also the mystical Jerusalem: the beautiful and perfect (or perfected) city of God, described as "coming down out of heaven as a bride adorned for her husband." It is shown in this vision to John to be a city resplendent with the glory of God, golden, bejewelled, and clear as crystal.

This wonderful vision of the New Jerusalem is a highlight in the Book of Revelation. It stands in sharp contrast to the dark realities of life with which so much of the book is concerned: the pain, sin, and distortion within God's good creation, those hard facts of living that are only too familiar to us who inhabit a broken world. In fact, while Saint John was writing about his vision of the New Jerusalem, most of the old Jerusalem, with which he had been familiar, lay in ruins, a sorry victim of Roman domination.

The images of the world that we view on our television screens are a bewildering contrast of ugliness and beauty. One minute people are in violent conflict, then comes David Attenborough showing us scenes of incomparable loveliness in the world of nature. So often (far too often in my opinion) nasty people do nasty things to other people. Yet we can sometimes watch scenes of tenderness and love that bring tears to the eyes.

## Hope

When darkness falls in our own lives, and we have to contend with personal sorrow, pain and loss, it is vital to have vision. How blest we are that our Christian Bible includes this vision given to John of the New Jerusalem. Out of all the turmoil of current affairs and human disarray comes this message of hope, of a "new heaven and a new earth", of a re-*newed* creation. And a message of God who judges all wickedness with total fairness, and who at, the same time, extends love and compassion, wiping the tears from eyes that are sore with weeping.

The earthly Jerusalem may be in ruins, our mortal bodies may have to be subject to pain and loss, and our hearts may have to cope with great sorrows. That is a necessary part of earthly existence. But it is far from being anything like the full story of creation, as Saint John so clearly saw. Jerusalem is the place, not only where Jesus had to undergo a painful death, but also where he was raised gloriously to triumph over all evil and death.

We live, as we must, in the old creation with all its pain and problems. But in the light of the resurrection of Christ we can already get a glimpse of the new, symbolised by the wonderful vision of the New Jerusalem. Today, the streets and sites of the city of Jerusalem seem confused and rough-and-ready sort of places. But the faithful pilgrim can see it all in spiritual terms, a city of perfect proportions, golden-paved, clear as crystal, pure as diamonds, beautiful as a bride on her wedding day: the city of God, and our true destination.

*The hymn by St Bernard, "Jerusalem the golden" is to be found in most hymn books.*

# God the Geometer
### Solihull Parish News May 2018

 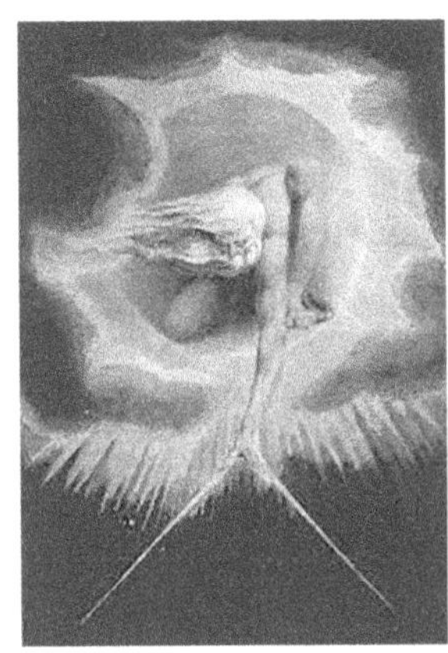

Look at these two strange pictures. The one on the left is an old Byzantine ikon: the other is a painting by William Blake, the 18th century mystic poet who wrote the hymn *Jerusalem (see next article)*. The paintings are best appreciated when viewed in colour in a book or on the Internet.

There are some curious words in Matthew 24.40, "One will be taken, the other left." They are a fragment from the apocalyptic writing that forms a part of Judaeo-Christian writing in the centuries before and after Christ. Meditating on this saying recently made me focus on the reality of division and separation as an inescapable part of what it is to be human. On the personal level, especially in one's latter years, bereavement is an obvious example, and dementia may well be another. But so too are estrangements and, on the broader canvas, the deep divisions between races and cultures, not to mention politicians.

Coming back now to the pictures. *God the Geometer* depicts the ancient symbol for God (i.e. old man with beard, though I must say he looks a good deal younger than William Blake's *Ancient of Days*). In both pictures, God is holding what, in my school geometry set, was called a "divider" or "pair of dividers", which is like a pair of compasses with two sharp points. The picture implies the traditional (or ancient mystical) view that in order to create, there has to be some kind of division or separation, neatly summed up in the old adage, "you can't make an omelette without breaking eggs."

I am finding it helpful to bear this in mind as I consider the current state of the world. With all the troubles and natural calamities, it seems as if the apocalyptic scenario in Matthew 24 is starting to happen in our own time. It is tempting to slip into this inaccurate mode of thinking, a stance that is often taken by Christian fundamentalists. The picture of God the Geometer corrects this misunderstanding, with its clear message that division is integrally a part of creation (see Isaiah 45.7). The so-called Prodigal Son *has* to separate himself from his home and discover pain and distress in order to "come to himself" (Luke 15.17), in other words, to find his true self. Only then can he experience the true joy of homecoming and understand the perfect loving of his Father. Somewhere concealed in these thoughts is to be found the meaning of pain and suffering, the cross of Jesus and the anguish of the world.

## Perfection

In the ikon, God the Geometer stands with the divider, but in creating the world (coincidentally bringing into being both space and time) he is also seen using the divider as a pair of compasses, circumscribing the globe. The circle stands for eternity and perfection. God sees creation as it is meant to be, perfect: as it says repeatedly in the first chapter of Genesis, "... and God saw that it was good."

The use of dividers also implies another basic and ancient mystical symbol, the triangle. We tend to think that the (triangular) notion of the Trinity is a purely Christian idea put together by the creed-makers during the early centuries of our religion. In fact it is part of spiritual geometry that reaches way back in time. For instance, put two equilateral triangles one inverted on top of the other, and you have the six-pointed Star of David. And in Genesis (18.2) one of the theophanies (showings of God) refers to not one, but three divine visitors. And this story is the subject of another famous ikon, *The Trinity* by Rublev (Russian 15th century).

I revere anyone who is good at maths. I had a lovely geometry set at school, but I wasn't much good at using it. I sometimes think of God as a supreme mathematician. So, it seems, did the wisdom of the ancient world. At the same time, I cannot believe that God has any interest in statistics, that addiction of the modern age. God surely counts in ones, not in groups or percentages. I feel sure that Stephen Hawking must be having some *very* interesting heavenly dialogues!

# Jerusalem the Hymn:
a personal view of a favourite hymn[8]
Solihull Parish News September 2015

In spite of my degree in English Literature, I have not yet been able to come to terms with the writings of William Blake. In some ways, he seems to be activated by the same kind of "romantic" spirit as Wordsworth, reacting against the formalism and rationalism of the previous hundred years and driven by a kind of visionary urgency to write large quantities of verse. Whereas Wordsworth's output is, for the most part, readily accessible, Blake's is often so obscure that one is left wondering whether it could ever be understood or interpreted, even by the writer himself. Yet, like Wordsworth, he was capable of producing lines of extraordinary childlike simplicity and beauty that set the spine tingling: *Little lamb who made thee... Tiger, tiger, burning bright ... Eternity in a grain of sand ...* and so on.

"And did those feet in ancient time" hovers between the simple and the obscure. The first verse of the hymn derives from the well-known legend of Joseph of Arimathea bringing a youthful Jesus to England. The story is embedded in the folklore of the West Country, focussed on Glastonbury, where it runs alongside the legends of King Arthur. Over the past 50 years, Glastonbury has become a New Age pilgrimage centre, now with an annual Music Festival that has reached mega-proportions. The town is currently full of "alternative" shops trading in magic and mystery, potions and crystals etc. England, of course, is not the only country to have claimed a visit from Jesus, but the New Testament will only allow for Egypt and Syro-Phoenicia.

The poem "And did those feet in ancient time" was written as a preface to a longer poem entitled "Milton" which was published towards the end of Blake's life in 1804. This preface, originally written as four short verses, only came into prominence during the First World War when, in 1916, the poet laureate Robert Bridges asked Sir Hubert Parry to set it to music so that it might become a patriotic song for the "Fight for the Right" movement. It was then appropriated at the end of the war by the suffragette

---

[8]  I am indebted to *The Penguin Book of Hymns* and to *Wikipedia* for information relating to Blake's poem.

movement as a kind of anthem, and subsequently taken up for that purpose by The Women's Institute movement during the 1920s. It was first set as a hymn in 1923 in the *Student Hymnal* using Parry's stirring tune. *The English Hymnal* originally located it in their appendix without a tune, a somewhat lowly location, possibly because some clergy were loth to consider it as a hymn at all. Since then, it has vastly increased in popularity, almost certainly because the tune seems perfectly to express the revolutionary ethos of the poem which encourages the building of a better world order.

## Revolutionary

Blake was a great admirer of John Milton, who lived and wrote 100 years earlier during the time of the Commonwealth in the 17th century. That indeed was a revolutionary era, driven by the ideal of reconstructing a society free from the depredations of incompetent monarchs and corrupt leadership. Blake was also a supporter of the French Revolution of his own time, which was motivated by similar ideals to the English Commonwealth.

This background helps us a little to understand the meaning of the last two verses of Blake's poem, which form the second verse of the hymn as we sing it. When it comes to detail, most people today would consider the "dark satanic mills" as referring to the shadow-side of the industrial revolution, with its overcrowded slums, polluting factories and workshops, and child labour. These conditions, apart from the child labour, were to be experienced in parts of England until the mid-20th century, so Blake can be thought of as an early champion in a long line of social reformers who battled all through the 19th and early 20th centuries for better living conditions for the under-privileged. His imagery is combative, with its sword, spear, bows and arrows, war chariot, and mental fight. Deriving from the Bible (one thinks of Paul's vivid picture of the Christian soldier, armed for the spiritual battle in Ephesians 6) such language abounds in the most popular hymns of the 19th and 20th centuries: *Onward Christian Soldiers (1864)*, and *Fight the Good Fight (1863)* are obvious examples.

Alternative interpretations have been offered. It has been suggested that the *dark satanic mills* might signify the rationalist and materialistic thought structures of the philosophy of the so-called *Age of Enlightenment*, against which the Romantic movement of the late 18th and early 19th centuries reacted so strongly. Another possibility is that Blake had in mind the hidebound structures of organised religion, whether pre- or post-Reformation, which allowed little room for the more mystical and esoteric religious experience favoured by Blake and many other "Romantics".

Be all that as it may, the hymn now commonly known as "Jerusalem" remains firmly among England's top ten favourite hymns, along with *Abide with Me*, *Morning has Broken*, and *Dear Lord and Father of Mankind*. It remains the anthem of the Womens' Institute movement, even though it may not be sung at every meeting held; and it still raises the roof of the Royal Albert Hall on the last night of the Promenade Concerts (as well as many other roofs of the pubs and other venues which either tune in to, or re-enact *The Last Night of the Proms* all over the country). I guess that most of those people who sing it with such fervour today don't think much about the words: they are simply feeling a natural empathy with Parry's glorious tune which seems perfectly to embrace the spirit of Blake's poem. I am sure that nearly all of the hymn's singers, whether in church or elsewhere, who *do* think about the words, and have some general knowledge, would have in mind the grim working conditions in the factories of 19th century England. All of us who love the hymn, including me, will at the very least be inspired by that highly successful marriage of words and music which urge us to look to, and to work and pray for, a brighter future for a world still struggling to overcome the evil forces of poverty, oppression, and the misuse of wealth and power.

***Llangasty Beacon, Wales***

Have you ever heard of Saint Gastyn? Few people have. This 5th century hermit would have slipped into obscurity except that his name became attached to the small Welsh village in Brecon which is located somewhere in the vicinity of where his hermitage used to be.

The old vicarage in Llangasty was converted into a retreat house in 1954. The tranquil scene in this sketch is the view from the sitting-room window. Can you imagine a better venue for peace, prayer, and meditation? The church and vicarage both have historic connections with the local Raikes family: Robert Raikes founded the Sunday School movement in the 18th century.

The lake is Llangors. At its southern end (out of sight of this view) is a PGL holiday centre. Their small colourful dinghies are sometimes seen skittering across the water like butterflies. The only other neighbours are occasional cattle in the nearby pasture, meditatively chewing the cud.

# CHAPTER SEVEN

# Holy Geography

## Promised Land
Solihull Parish News June 2011

When we read the Bible we are given to understand that God set aside a small fragment of the earth's surface as a specific location or homeland for His chosen people, the Jews. This idea is one of the strongest themes in the Old Testament. It strides across book after book. The Promised Land is the focus of hope for God's people, celebrated in ritual and poetry and song, lamented when it is violated or overrun by foreigners, cherished when re-occupied by Jews, continually mourned by the Jewish *diaspora* for the best part of twenty centuries from the first to the twentieth until finally re-established as a political entity in 1948.

For Jews, the Promised Land is the place where the Messiah, God's anointed saviour of the Jews, will be revealed. For Christians it is the birthplace, and death-and-resurrection place of the Messiah identified as Jesus, the Saviour of all humankind. For Muslims, too, the land is sacred within the memory of God's prophet Mohammed who, in Muslim estimation, stands in stature alongside Abraham and Jesus as one of God's specially chosen and favoured ones.

The big question for us is how Christians should interpret this promise. It was clear from its beginnings that the Christian religion had a worldwide message and mission, so any idea of geographical limitation to God's kingdom was no longer valid. In Christian devotion as well as in theology, it has always been considered that the inspired scriptures that constitute our Bible, in particular the scriptures of the Old Testament, bear a meaning and significance far beyond the literal sense of the words. This is especially true of the narratives about the Exodus and subsequent settlement in the land of Canaan. The great themes of deliverance and freedom, of pilgrimage and promise, of temptation and sin and forgiveness, of divine guidance and providence, and many others are all contained in and illuminated by the stories of Exodus, as they are once again in the narrating and understanding of the later Babylonian Exile. In

Christian interpretation, they slot into the drama of Holy Week and Easter, and resonate in our liturgy as we celebrate and reflect on the meaning of salvation, deliverance, judgement and eternal life.

In this context, the whole idea of the Promised Land has been given a new and creative interpretation expressed most clearly in our hymnody, and just as persuasively in the spirituals sung by the black slaves in the 19th century. A prime example is the hymn *Guide me O thou great Redeemer:*

> *When I tread the verge of Jordan, bid my anxious fears subside;*
> *Death of death, and hell's destruction, land me safe on Canaan's side.*

or the spiritual *Deep River.*

> *Deep river, my heart is over Jordan;*
> *Deep river, I want to cross over into camp ground.*
> *O don't you want to go to that Gospel feast,*
> *That promised land where all is peace.*

The Promised Land has now become Heaven or Paradise which, in most Christian theologies, is that spiritual home which awaits us after death, though some sects (notably Jehovah's Witnesses) consider this blessed state as occurring on this planet at some future date.

In spite of this, an astonishing number of people, non-Jews as well as Jewish, still choose to interpret the scriptures literally. The creation of the Israeli state in 1948 inevitably reinforced this literalism. I believe that this is retrograde thinking, which can only exacerbate and prolong the propensity for political turmoil that has been the hallmark of the inhabitants of the homeland of Jesus for so many centuries. I also reckon that the time has come to reinterpret the concept of Promised Land, but this time thinking in global terms.

## Sacred Space

Why should the Promised Land not be, in fact, this planet earth in its entirety? In the Bible the Promised Land is depicted as a place "flowing with milk and honey". It is lavishly endowed, a place where there is room for all God's people with a sufficiency of resources to meet all the necessities of life. This is clearly not the case in that small strip of land bordering the East Mediterranean, nor can it ever be. This planet earth, on the other hand, precisely meets those criteria of space and adequate provision for God's people, and I am taking "God's people" to mean the sum total of human beings alive at any one period of time. The fact that we are constantly faced with world shortages is almost entirely due to imbalance in the global economy, and that is entirely the fault of sinful human beings and the institutions and systems that we create and sustain which are engineered to satisfy greed rather than provide for need.

A key text from the Old Testament is to be found in Exodus chapter 3. This is the story of the burning bush, the encounter between Moses and God when Moses hears God's voice declaring, "the place on which you are standing is holy ground" (verse 5). Outwardly, there is nothing to distinguish this piece of land from any other, and it is significantly situated outside the borders of Israel/Palestine. We should consider those words as spoken to human beings wherever they are. The ground beneath our feet is holy ground, holy land, created by God for humanity. Psalm 24 declares "The earth is the Lord's and all that therein is: the compass of the world and they that dwell therein" (verse 1). Traditional wisdom teaches that human beings are the crown of God's creation and God's vice-regents appointed to care for this sacred earth. And biblical theology echoes this teaching in the book Genesis 2.15: "And the Lord God took the man and put him in the garden of Eden to till it and look after it." It is evident that human beings are placed here to care for our holy land in all its richness and diversity and beauty.

The contemporary concern for the environment is a tiny step in the right direction and deserves all the encouragement that we can give it. But at present it has nowhere near sufficient impetus and support to counteract the systemic failure of the modern world in its extravagance and catastrophic exploitation of the planet's resources.

The people who live in Israel/Palestine are living on land that is no more, nor less, holy than the land I am now standing on. Yet whoever they may be, in any age or generation, they should consider themselves as guardians of a special piece of territory, which can act as a constant "visual aid" for people of faith. The homeland of Jesus must remain a place of pilgrimage for all nations. But for our part, let us never forget that the land of God's promise is this precious globe. We will never, nor need we ever, transform it into a heaven-on-earth, but we must try to recognise it as a foretaste of heaven, sacred space, a holy land where human beings have the opportunity to prepare for the greater life which is destined for us beyond this life and this planet.

# Sacred Geography
Solihull Parish News July 2012

The two pilgrimages to the Holy Land that I made during the 1970s and 1980s left me with the profound impression that the places I visited were special. If one goes to Israel/Palestine as a pilgrim and not simply as a tourist, then one cannot come away without having been greatly moved by the experience. The Bible comes alive in a most amazing way. For a lifelong Christian, to be where Jesus was, see what he saw, and walk where he once trod, raises such powerful emotions as to reduce one to tears of joy.

Over the years, I have often been able to share this great experience when showing my slides. I have always ended the talk with a final picture of a simple waterside scene: a lake with a small stony beach. It is a snap that could have been taken in countless places around the world. In the foreground can be seen the remains of a small open fire with a few dying embers. The location is the Sea of Galilee near Capernaum, the place where, after his resurrection, Jesus appeared on the shore to some of his fishermen-disciples as they were in their boat on the nearby waters. The fire, left by some previous visitors, brought vividly to mind the simple meal that Jesus had shared with his friends. You can read about it in the 21st chapter of John's Gospel.

In my comments about that particular slide, I point out that there is nothing especially holy about that piece of ground, for surely all ground is holy to those who believe in God, wherever you happen to be. "In His hand are <u>all</u> the corners of the earth" (Psalm 95). Looking at the Holy Land from this standpoint, one cannot but be grieved by the incessant and continuing conflict which has been the hallmark of Palestine down the centuries and which has shamefully escalated in our own times. This I believe to be largely the result of a radical misunderstanding of the Bible, driven by fundamentalism. It is true that the Jewish scriptures of the Old Testament make a compelling case for considering the territory we call the Holy Land as a tract of land promised by God to be a homeland for the twelve tribes of Israel. But that understanding depends on a purely literal interpretation of the Bible. There are two important arguments that can be used to refute the Zionist claim.

First, a balanced <u>historical</u> appraisal of the texts reveals that they were written and edited with a very definite aim to reinforce and protect the territorial conquests of the migratory tribes who had chosen to settle in that area during the first millennium BC. Second, a balanced <u>theological</u> appraisal of the Old Testament clearly finds an emphasis, not on the occupation of a specific tract of land, but on the careful preparation of a people chosen by God to become the right context for the coming of the Messiah. So the land is a purely incidental background to the dramatic story of a people being trained in holiness so that they could be ready for the appearance of the Saviour of the world, the coming of Jesus, God's anointed one, the Messiah/Christ.

## Jubilee Year

It is evident from the Christian scriptures of the New Testament that, with the coming of Jesus and the consequent arrival of the Spirit-Community known as the Church, concerns about tribal territory become an irrelevance. The first Christian missionaries, especially Saint Paul, recognised this straight away. But subsequent generations have been slow to understand the far-reaching implications of this salvation message. One of these implications is the assertion I made earlier: that <u>ALL</u> ground, land, or territory is holy. Wherever you are, you are standing on holy ground. We desperately need this understanding today, for an unholy alliance between secularists and technocrats has brought us to the brink of an environmental and ecological crisis of vast proportions which threatens the survival of the human race on our planet.

Interestingly, the Jewish scriptures themselves provide a strong counterpoint to the sadly misunderstood theme of the Promised Land. It is to be found in the Law of Moses, in chapter 25 of the book Leviticus. The writer is explaining the concept of the Jubilee Year, a complicated economic programme of debt remission and returning of purchased land, which may have had some relevance for a primitive tribal culture but is totally impractical in any other context. But the key statement comes in verse 23, when God says categorically, "The land belongs to ME. You are only temporary sojourners and tenants." This saying finds echoes in other parts of the Bible (Exodus 9.29; 19.5: Deuteronomy 10.14: 1 Chronicles 29.11: Psalms 24.1; 50.12; 89.11).

In light of this, I cannot help thinking that the current situation in the Holy Land is due to an anachronism based on a misreading of the text and a blinkered fundamentalist understanding of the Bible and the

Koran. Our sacred scriptures have always been rightly subject to a spiritual interpretation so that they may be understood in terms of myth and symbol and imagery. This finds expression in Christian liturgies and hymnody, whereby we can adopt and live by a reinterpretation of the biblical ideas of exodus and exile, of slavery and freedom, of war and peace, and of course of promised land:

> *When I tread the verge of Jordan*
> *Bid my anxious fears subside,*
> *Death of death and hell's destruction*
> *Land me safe on Canaan's side.*

This is not an expression of territorial longing: it is sacred geography. The literalist and fundamentalist stance, adopted by Zionists and Islamists (and also by much of Western evangelical Christianity), which currently drives the politics of the Middle East can only lead to an exacerbation of the tragic circumstances that we are witnessing there and elsewhere.

—◄◦►—

# Politics and Religion
### Solihull Parish News February 2010

On the Sunday before Easter, Palm Sunday, Christians recall the event of Jesus' entry into Jerusalem, riding on a donkey, to the acclamation of the crowds. We note that he rides on a humble beast of burden, but the crowds shout "Hosanna to the Son of David!" Those words are effectively a coronation. They put on to Jesus a label, King Messiah, the saviour of the nation.

On that first Palm Sunday there were, in fact, not one, but two processions going into Jerusalem. From the East came Jesus on the donkey, surrounded mostly by the working classes. From the West came the Roman Governor, Pontius Pilatus, resplendent, surrounded by a cohort of armed soldiers, securely seated on their warhorses, eight feet above the rabble. Pilate was riding, probably with bad grace, into the hot and dusty capital city from his pleasant seaside villa in Caesarea, to supervise the security arrangements for the Jewish Passover festival. He represented his god, who was the emperor of Rome. He anticipated trouble and, at this time of the year, often got it. He was prepared if necessary to deal with it summarily.

Five days later, in the early morning, the principal players in these two royal processions met, for the first and last time. The most interesting account of that encounter is to be found in the eighteenth chapter of Saint John's Gospel. It contains the enigmatic words from Jesus, "My kingdom is not of this world."

## Challenge

It has been a favourite opinion among English people that "religion and politics don't mix". In these days it is being called into question: witness the occasional public discussion on whether politicians should or should not "do God". A little reflection reveals that the statement "religion and politics don't mix" is about as shallow as the Dogger Bank at low tide. There is, however, an element of truth in it. When religion and politics interconnect in such a way that you cannot distinguish any dividing line between them, as in a theocracy, then that can very easily lead to intolerance and spell trouble. We have seen that happen close to home in Northern Ireland: and we currently see it happening in the Middle East and in the northwest region of the Indian sub-continent.

Simply to say categorically that religion and politics don't mix makes little sense without indicating more clearly what you really mean. The statement is often no more than a thoughtless reaction from politicians and others in influential positions. Those who use it are usually indicating that they cannot bear to have their systems and policies and cherished ideas scrutinised and challenged. They tend to get very hot under the collar if their critics are God-fearing people who are clearly on the side of the poor and marginalised folk in society, as Jesus was. That is when you hear people saying "bishops shouldn't meddle in politics."

Some Christians, worried perhaps about some of the lethal side-effects of politicised religion, prefer to keep religion and politics firmly separated. Caution is needed that this doesn't become an excuse to 'privatise' religion. English Christians have often been too ready to proclaim, "my religion is my private affair, something between me and God that I would rather not talk about: something that I prefer to keep separate from what I think and do day by day." That really is not good quality religion.

When Jesus said to Pilate: "My kingdom is not of this world", he was certainly not building an impenetrable wall between the world of the spirit and the world of every day. He could hardly do that, because he himself was the embodiment of the unity of heaven and earth. Saint John made that clear when he introduced Jesus as the Word (of God) made flesh and dwelling among us. Confronting Pilate, Jesus was pointing out to a hard-bitten military politician the existence and real importance of the spiritual dimension. He was attempting to convey to a man of power that you cannot reduce the created world, and human beings within it, to a kind of automated machine that can be run and manipulated by clever political mechanics, or by military might, or even by state-of-the-art technology. That is just as much a lesson for our day as it was for Pontius Pilate.

## Make Space

At the same time, Jesus was making it clear that there is indeed a proper distinction between religion and politics, and that there needs to be space between them. That is what he meant when he memorably said earlier on, "Render to Caesar the things that are Caesar's, and to God the things that are God's". As a citizen he knew that there had to be systems and organisation, both social and political, to enable human beings to live creatively with each other. He also saw very clearly what many of the other religious leaders of his day were blind to: it is bad news when religion and politics become enmeshed together and ignore the space they need between them.

The poignancy of that meeting between Jesus and Pilate suddenly makes itself felt. Pilate was obviously impressed by Jesus, even though he couldn't understand him. So he pronounced him innocent, and initially ordered his release. But the system of the time prevailed. The politicised priesthood secured the death of Jesus as a subversive, which of course in a sense he was, and still is.

"My kingdom is not of this world" does not mean that the kingdom of God, to which Christians belong, is some other-worldly, detached arena where we can happily do religious things and forget about the cares and responsibilities of everyday life. It does mean that we are firmly embedded in both the spiritual *and* the material worlds. They are two modes of being that are equally real, true, and significant. Each must be taken into account day by day, and each must influence and inform the other.

To belong to God's kingdom means that we are called, as Jesus was, to love and enhance in ourselves the authentic Christian values of love, peace, reconciliation, joy, self-discipline and truth. We must also bring these values to bear on the life we lead in society. It also means that, as disciples of Christ, we should be prepared to challenge the accepted values of the society we live in, whenever these values are based on selfish gain, exploitation, personal enhancement at other people's expense, and easy excuses for low moral standards.

By way of a postscript: it is interesting to note that the politicised Judaism of Jesus' day was demolished under Roman rule just forty years after his death and resurrection.[9] Eventually, as we know, Rome itself with all its might declined and fell. The kingdom of God, however, which Jesus spoke about and embodied, began to spread both deeply and widely in human consciousness from his own day onwards.

Christians rejoice at this but cannot be complacent. The political and economic kingdoms of the world are powerful, and often powerfully resistant to the kingdom of God and all that it stands for. In a sense, Jesus still stands before Pilate. We stand there too, and it seems right to end by posing a cliff-hanging question: which side are we really on?

---

[9]  In modern times attempts are constantly being made to revive it.

**St Andrew's, Worcester**

Irresistible to a sketcher, the slim and elegant spire of St Andrew's demands to be drawn. It also demands to be questioned.

Question 1. Where's the church? At this distance you can't see it. Go closer and you still won't see it, Why? Because it isn't there! The tower and spire stand alone in an attractive public garden. The church was given to the city by the Bishop in 1940. Apart from the tower and spire, it was demolished around 1949 together with the slum dwellings that surrounded it. The building had become as dilapidated as the poor houses and was a sad relic, crumbling in a parish just five acres in extent, with neither building nor parish being any longer fit for purpose.

Question 2. What is the connection with a Tudor stately home situated 25 miles away near Winchcombe? (Clue: the spire is affectionately known by the citizens of Worcester as "The Glovers Needle"). During the 19$^{th}$ century, glove-making was a principal manufacturing enterprise in the city. In 1837, two wealthy "glovers", the brothers John and William Dent, respected Worcester residents and benefactors in their day, acquired the semi-ruinous Tudor Sudeley Castle (best known for its association with

Henry VIII's surviving wife Katherine Parr) and began the process of its restoration. A single one-ton bell remains in the tower of St Andrew's. It tolls solemnly twice a year, summoning the worthy town councillors to their plenary meetings. Recently a clock has been installed as a millennium project, and the RNIB have been permitted to place a camcorder in a lofty position where peregrine falcons are wont to make their nests.

*Note:* I am grateful to Wikipedia for some of the information above.

# CHAPTER EIGHT

# *Jesus, man and boy*

## Jesus and Politics
### Solihull Parish News October 2005

At the end of the Christian year, on the Sunday before Advent, the Church keeps the festival of Christ the King. It is good that we have this opportunity to celebrate our faith triumphantly, to declare in songs of praise and thanksgiving that Jesus Christ is sovereign Lord of all.

The Gospel reading, however (John 18. 33-37: Jesus before Pilate), should give us pause for thought. In fact, it should stop us in our tracks. For Saint John is not presenting us with a royal personage on display with all the trappings of sovereignty. Quite the contrary! Imagine yourself standing beside Pontius Pilate the governor. You are faced with a sorry-looking sight: a prisoner, bedraggled and helpless, bearing the marks of a night of brutal interrogation, waiting for the death penalty. If anyone is regal in this setting, it is surely Pilatus, the imperial governor, who rules the land with the emperor's authority, backed up by the military might of the empire of Rome. Yet Saint John makes it clear, as he carefully represents the dialogue between the two men, that we are to reconsider the whole scenario (John 18.33-38 abbreviated):

"Are you the king of the Jews?" asks Pilate, with raised eyebrows. The Greek makes it clear that the emphasis is on the pronoun: "Are you the king of the Jews?"

Jesus replies with another question: "Are you asking this off your own bat, or because of what other people are saying?"

"What have you done?" Pilate responds. Jesus' reply is direct, but puzzling: "My kingdom does not belong to this world".

Pilate replies, almost jokingly, but not quite, because he is still puzzled. "You're not a <u>real</u> king, are you?"

He is both astonished and exasperated when his prisoner replies: "This is why I came into the world, to testify to the truth."

This is nothing like the deferential and hopeless attitude of a beaten prisoner. We are really being invited to consider who the judge is and who the prisoner is. Where does the real sovereign power lie? Is it with Pilatus, who is bound by the role he has to fulfil as governor, or is it with Jesus, who is blatantly innocent, gloriously free from guilt, and with his integrity totally intact? In effect, the tables have turned. Pontius Pilate remains no more than a nasty taste in history, whereas the glory of Jesus, conqueror of death, has filled the world forever with light and love. Yet the very concept of Christ as King also raises some deep and searching questions about the interface between religion and politics.

In Jesus' day, and long before, and ever since, religion and politics have been so inextricably mixed that it is not possible to see where the one ends and the other begins. If we lived in an ideal world, peopled by perfect beings, this would never be a problem, because the love of God would be perfectly mirrored in the love of each human being for one another. But such a garden of Eden has never really existed. If Eden exists in any sense at all, it is in the future, not the past.

Instead, it is in the nature of things that we must accept cost and conflict. These are the growing pains of humankind as we grow towards the perfect kingdom of God that is our destiny. That is why religion must work hand in hand with politics, and at the same time, must apply a critique for political and other institutions, including its own. As he stands before Pilate, Jesus is doing just this. He is drawing an enormous question mark over the politics and the religious institutions of his day, both of which were capable of putting to death a totally innocent person.

Where, then, do we stand, we who acknowledge Christ as King?

As human beings, however much we may want to live private lives as individuals, we must live collectively in society. To do this, we must find a way in which sovereignty and authority can be arranged to everyone's advantage. This is a big struggle. As Christians, we can in no way contract out of this responsibility. We are part of political life, and therefore we must engage in it according to our ability, at the very least by exercising our right to vote in elections.

As Christians, however, we have an *added* responsibility. That is, to ensure by prayer and action, that the spiritual, the divine dimension, is never left out of politics and political decision-making. Like Jesus before Pilate, we stand before society as witnesses to the truths of God as they are revealed in Holy Scripture and by holy people. But we must never forget that we can have no justification for doing this, unless and until we have enthroned Jesus as Lord in our own hearts. That is the core meaning of the doctrine of Christ the King, the enthronement of Jesus in our hearts as the king of love who rules our lives. These words from the hymn *At the name of Jesus* are apt and relevant:

> In your hearts enthrone him,
> There let him subdue
> All that is *not* holy,
> All that is *not* true.

Without Jesus enthroned in our hearts, we have no real authority to challenge anything, whether injustice, or crime, or falsehood, or even bad behaviour. Without him, all we can do is moan, complain, be petulant and ineffective, and nothing will change.

By contrast, if Christ is truly enthroned within us, and we are *totally* loyal to him and all that he stands for in the Gospel, then we shall have the spiritual authority to discern what is counterfeit and fraudulent in our society, and to challenge and engage in an effective battle against all kinds of evil. In this way, whether by prayer or action or both, we shall be sharing in the sovereignty and dominion of Christ who is our Lord and King. And we shall be doing our bit to bring about that for which we pray, when we say "Thy kingdom come, thy will be done, on earth as it is in heaven".

# Jesus the Adolescent

Solihull Parish News February 2013

*In this article I am taking a brief glance at a neglected stage in the life of Jesus. If you have not visited the Holy Land, I would suggest that a large-scale map of Israel/Palestine and a bit of Internet "Googling" would be an advantage.*

One of the churches in Nazareth is dedicated to Jesus the Adolescent, an unusual, perhaps unique dedication.

At the start of the year, in the Christian calendar, we leap from thinking about Jesus as an infant straight into his adult life, with only the episode of his being 'lost' in Jerusalem at the age of twelve stuck in between. To consider and meditate on Jesus as an adolescent growing up in and around Nazareth will help us to have a rounder picture of our Saviour. I must admit that this was much easier for me after I had been on pilgrimage to the Holy Land.

Today, Nazareth is a modern town of about 60,000 inhabitants many of whom are Christian. In Jesus' time it was no more than a small village of a few hundred people, built on sloping ground. In such a place, the carpenter would have been a villager of some consequence, and never short of work. The presumed site of the premises of Joseph's carpentry business is to be found below the Church of St Joseph. It is just an excavated cave, which must have been behind the small modest working-class home once occupied by the Holy Family.

It was customary for ordinary people in the first century to build their houses in front of a hillside cave, which would then be an integral part of the living and working space. From the early centuries, pilgrims to Nazareth have been shown the place where the Holy Family lived. Although ground levels have changed with the passing of centuries, there seems no reason to doubt that this grotto is the place where Jesus was brought up with his family.

Pilgrims in Nazareth can also visit "Mary's Well". Strictly speaking, this shrine is not a well at all. The water supply for Nazareth came from a rocky spring in the hillside, and was taken by conduit to some kind of container from which the villagers, including Jesus's mother, would come to collect it. Such water supplies are not generally subject to change, so this could count as one of the relatively few truly authentic sites in the Holy Land. The modern construction at Mary's Well is a Greek Orthodox sanctuary, for the Orthodox Church believes that the visit of the arch-angel Gabriel to Mary happened while Mary was collecting water.

Judging from the story of the twelve-year-old Jesus in the Temple (which can be found in Luke's Gospel (chapter 2 verse 41), he must have been an adventurous as well as an intelligent lad. I can imagine Jesus, alone or with friends, roaming the Galilean countryside much as I did the North Yorkshire moors during school holidays. Take a good day's walk from Nazareth in a northeasterly direction and you come to the Sea of Tiberias (Yam Kinneret on today's maps, the biblical Gennesaret). I feel sure that Jesus must often have gone there as a boy and played on the shore. Doubtless he made friends with the local fishermen and their children. On his days off from the synagogue school and the carpenter's shop, Jesus could have walked from Nazareth to the top of Mount Tabor. From its summit he would have had a magnificent view of the surround-ing countryside and across the north of Israel almost as far as the Great Sea (Mediterranean). There is no place like the top of a mountain (even a small one like this) for inspiration and prayer. Thirty years later, in the sight of his closest companions, it was here where Jesus shone with the mysterious light of God (Matthew 17. 1-8).

A large proportion of Jesus's fellow-countrymen didn't live in settled accommodation as he did with his family. They were "travellers", Bedouin people who lived in tents made out of animal hide. There are plenty of them today in Palestine living in tents that must look very similar to those of their remote ancestors, except for the accompanying TV aerial and satellite dish. The Bedouin often make their living by shepherding. Jesus must surely have spent some time as a boy in close proximity to shepherds and their sheep, living the $23^{rd}$ Psalm, as he wandered around the Gali-lean countryside. Sometimes the Bedouin leave pale-coloured round loaves of bread to rise in the warmth of the sun. Jesus was obviously reminded of these when he was tempted by the Devil to turn one of the round white stones of the Judaean desert into a loaf.

## Jerusalem

It takes at least three days' walking to get to Jerusalem from Nazareth. It is possible that Jesus's parents went there each year for a Jewish religious festival and took the family with them. I remember, when I was in Jerusa-lem, watching a boy across the street, carrying a satchel on his way to school. I thought of Jesus, about the same age, wandering off to the

Temple when he should have been with his family on their way back north. For them, he was a small boy lost in the city of Jerusalem. In reality, he was no more 'lost' than this small boy in a street in today's Jerusalem, on his way to school. Like him, Jesus was looking for instruction.

Herod's Temple in Jerusalem, as Jesus would have known it, was absolutely stunning. To get some idea of its size, you need to realise the height of the central structure as equivalent to that of a sizeable English country church tower *and* spire, and its precincts extending over several acres. With its construction in gleaming white marble and gilt adornment, it is not surprising that it counted as one of the seven wonders of the ancient world. You can readily imagine the impression it must have made on visitors and pilgrims, not least on a boy of twelve, coming here for his Bar-Mitzvah ceremony as Jesus probably was.

Put an adult human being beside one of the pillars in the temple colonnade and he might measure about one-tenth of its height. In the days of Jesus, it was in the colonnade, in the open air, that the learned Doctors of Religion taught their students in groups of varying numbers. The young men would choose which teacher they preferred, and Jesus, 'newly-confirmed' we might say, spent a couple of days trying to find a suitable one. That might not have mattered, except that he was only 12 and had given his frantic relatives and friends the slip as he responded to what he felt to be a call from God. Thirty years later, as a highly unconventional rabbi himself, Jesus turned the system round and himself chose his followers.

I was helped to picture Jesus as an adolescent when I read a novel called *My Name was Judas* by C.K. Stead. In this book, Judas the betrayer is depicted as Jesus' best friend from childhood. Stead sees Judas as an only child from a privileged background and a rather starchy domestic environment who finds the rough and tumble of a working-class home in Nazareth an appealing alternative to his own home. In adolescence Jesus is shown as being intelligent, disturbingly unpredictable and moody, given to the occasional fit of anger and abuse. I know this is a novel and 'made up', but is that not rather a true picture of an adolescent? Perhaps these reflections will add a little colour to our Lent meditations.

# Here is a man
## Solihull Parish News July/August 2013

First, a quotation from an anonymous writer who lived over 300 years ago.

"Here is a man who was born in an obscure village, the child of a peasant woman. He worked in a carpenter's shop until he was thirty, and then for three years he was an itinerant preacher. He had no credentials but himself. While still a young man, the tide of popular opinion turned against him. His friends, the twelve men who had learned so much from him and had promised him their enduring loyalty, ran away and left him. He went through a mockery of a trial: he was nailed on a cross between two thieves. When he was dead, he was taken down and laid in a borrowed grave through the pity of a friend. Yet I am well within the mark when I say that all the armies that ever marched, and all the parliaments that ever sat, and all the kings that ever reigned, put together, have not affected the life of man upon this earth as has this one solitary life."

Visiting Hereford Cathedral many years ago, I picked up the visitors' leaflet "Welcome to Hereford Cathedral". It contained basic but useful information about what to look out for as you went round. It listed the daily and Sunday services and told you who to ask if you wanted to talk to someone. It also included the above quotation, which I thought was compelling in a simple and straightforward way. We know immediately, of course, who the "Man" is. Was it possible, I asked myself, that some of the visitors to the cathedral might in fact not know who the "Man" was?" If that were the case, perhaps they would ask one of the cathedral staff. I could imagine the visitor being told, "Well, if it wasn't for this man, whose name, by the way, is Jesus of Nazareth, this building would not be here, nor would the forty or so other cathedrals in this kingdom, nor would any of the churches that you see dotted about the English landscape…". So it might go on, and what a wonderful opportunity would be given to convey the good news which the leaflet hints at, of the resurrection of this same Jesus and the message of salvation promised by God through faith in him.

The value of our cathedrals and other notable church buildings in terms of cultural heritage cannot be denied. They may well, and often do, pose heavy problems for those who are responsible for their upkeep.

I suppose that, when our present civilization eventually (as it must) comes to its end, these splendid buildings will have crumbled to remnants of rubble and dust, and future archaeologists (if such people still exist) will painstakingly unearth the remains and try to interpret the story they have to tell, just as we do with the stones and bones of the past beneath our feet today.

Meanwhile, in the here and now, our splendid ancient churches still have a vital part to play in Christian witness and outreach. Their architecture and artefacts illuminate our study and understanding of society over many centuries, rather as the illuminations on an ancient manuscript enhance and enrich the written text. But more than that, our churches and cathedrals are still powerhouses of daily prayer and intercession as well as eloquent witnesses to the love of God shown in Jesus Christ. I am continually impressed, when I visit what some people sadly regard as little more than ancient monuments, by the visible signs of real spiritual life and Christian endeavour evident in the displays and notice boards. Impressed, because all this spiritual energy and dedication is happening in addition to (and in spite of) the massive task of maintenance and upkeep. There seems to me to be a creative tension at work here between two agendas, the spiritual and the monumental. This is surely part of the meaning of *incarnation*, the Word becoming flesh, a marriage of the spiritual and the material. Any viable church building has to be experienced as a meeting place between earth and heaven.

## Holy Temple

The creative tension of this 'meeting' was brought home to me vividly when, in July 2010, I presided at the 12 o'clock Saturday Eucharist in York Minster. My family and I were celebrating 100 years of ordained ministry in the Church of England from when my father was ordained in the Minster in 1910, continuing with my own ordination in Birmingham in 1960. During that service, it was sometimes hard to focus on the spiritual, having perforce to have entered the Minster via turnstiles, and then performing the liturgy while tourists (including a rather noisy bunch of Italian youths) continued their perambulations. Quieter reflection after the event helped me to realize that all these things are part of the total Christian ministry and witness, each having its particular focus, yet all in some way contributing to the earthly/heavenly experience for those in the building at the time.

The text for my sermon on that occasion came from Ephesians 2 verse
21 "The whole structure … grows into a holy temple." This is part of
what I had to say:

> Perhaps the sensation of shrinking came upon you as you entered this
> magnificent temple of the Lord. Perhaps, in part, this was the inten-
> tion of the builders of our cathedrals. These splendid temples are
> reminders of the awesome majesty of God who is all-beauty, as well as
> all-goodness and all-truth. At the same time, they cut us down to size,
> pointing the contrast between God's eternal greatness and our human
> fragility and littleness …

And the closing words of the sermon tie in with what I am trying to say in
this article about the vital relationship between the material and the spiritual:

> Humanity is in the process of being built by God into a holy temple.
> Imagine this Minster in the process of building: scaffolding, rubble, a
> mess of bits and pieces, masons cutting huge chunks of stone down to
> size, mistakes being made, accidents happening: beauty and ugliness
> side by side.
>
> God's gift of ministry, like the gift of faith, is being enabled to work on
> the building-site of human endeavour with all its apparent disorder,
> and never to lose sight of the potential, the process, and ultimately the
> glory of the completed temple.
>
> I just want to finish by sharing with you one of my favourite prayers.
> The analogy changes slightly, from construction to carpentry. But the
> general purpose of the prayer is very much along the same lines. After
> all, carpentry, like masonry, is very much a feature of church buildings.
>
> The prayer calls to mind Jesus at work in the carpenter's shop in Naza-
> reth, cutting pieces of wood down to size. And it also remembers how
> we are all saved by means of the squalid carpentry of his *Cross*.

Lord Jesus,
Master Carpenter of Nazareth,
who on the Cross through wood and nails
did work our whole salvation;
wield well the tools in this your workshop,
that we who come to you rough hewn
may by your hand
be fashioned to a truer beauty
and a greater usefulness;
for the honour of your Holy Name;
Amen.

**St Margaret's Church, Underriver, Kent**

I include this pen-and-ink sketch not for its excellence: that should be obvious! The building itself is a fair representation, but it looks as though it is half surrounded by boulders, or possibly flooded. Actually, that's a hedge along the front, enclosing the churchyard. And the tree is not growing on the roof but situated in the background.

However, I have a certain affection for the drawing because I used it among others to illustrate my book *Spirit and Life*, which was published in 1988. The book is the biography of Robert Coulson who founded The Fellowship of Contemplative Prayer in 1949. He was ordained as deacon, rather to his own surprise, in the diocese of Rochester in 1945 and the bishop then immediately put him in charge of the parish of Underriver in Kent even though he had to hire a priest to celebrate Holy Communion and take weddings until Robert was ordained priest three months later.

The story of my "conversion" from reluctant scribbler to book illustrator is told in *The Last of the Bluebells* which I published privately in 2011. It all happened within one year, greatly to my own astonishment. It was the result of my dear wife Irene's insistence that I go with her to art classes on Monday mornings, which, to begin with, I hated, until suddenly I "saw the light." The account of my other conversion (to contemplative prayer as a result of meeting Robert Coulson) is to be found in the biography.

# CHAPTER NINE

# *Some people*

## Brother Edward
Temple Balsall Church Magazine 2008

The history of Temple Balsall is dominated by its Templar connections, which is only natural considering the name and medieval associations. There is, however, a lesser-known but important piece of 20<sup>th</sup>-century church history attached to The Temple that deserves attention. This is the fourteen-year span from 1915 to 1929 when it was home to the dedicated and saintly, yet largely forgotten, evangelist extraordinaire known as Brother Edward. His full name was Edward Gordon Bulstrode; he was born in 1885 and died in 1953.

Ordained as an Anglican priest in 1910 at St Albans, Brother Edward felt strongly called to a special ministry of evangelism, particularly among the slum-dwelling poor of England's industrial cities. In later years he was to turn his attention to the countryside, and he founded the loose-knit community known as The Village Evangelists just after the Second World War. His earlier association with Temple Balsall stood him in good stead in this latter phase of his roving ministry.

From 1915 to 1929 Brother Edward used Temple Balsall as a spiritual base and powerhouse from which he could respond to calls to lead parish missions and retreats all over the country. His calling led him to a rather solitary career, which was sometimes hard to come to terms with having been brought up in a devout and loving family as the youngest of 14 children. He consequently valued very highly both the spiritual and domestic environment at Temple Balsall, which he called his "second home" during these 14 years. The incumbent at the time was the Revd. Frank Fairbairn whose devout and diminutive wife Sophia (she used to say she had been baptised in a sugar basin) mothered Brother Edward both materially and spiritually. Brother Edward and those whom he inspired and who worked with him made a considerable impact in the many parishes to which they were invited, preaching the Gospel, very often to the un-churched, and encouraging both clergy and laity in their faith.

## Reforming Worship

Also closely connected with Temple Balsall is another important development in the history of the Church of England during the 20th century that has transformed the church life and worship of practically every parish in the country. This is The Parish Communion, which began to be widely accepted in many parishes as the principal service on a Sunday morning, in place of 11 o'clock Mattins. This *gathering of the Lord's Own People around the Lord's Own Table on the Lord's Own Day* is something that most of us now take for granted. But it did not really become commonplace until the 1960s. However, its roots go back a long way. Among the very few churches where it was pioneered was Temple Balsall, where it was a key factor in a mission undertaken there by a Mirfield Father, Fr. Seyzinger, in 1913. This was just two years before Brother Edward moved in. This is how the experiment is (somewhat romantically) described by the vicar, Frank Fairbairn:

*The service, which lasts an hour, is congregational throughout, and well interspersed with hymns, and the people come to it from all corners of the parish. The Eucharist was offered in, for, and by the whole family of the faithful of the Household of Faith Sunday by Sunday. The people were their own choir. They sang Merbecke, and did not tire of him, and 'a very little musical talent went, by the blessing of God, a long way'. Everything was done to emphasize that this was the characteristic act of worship of a family. The notices and biddings were of simple homely things, causes, and persons – known to all and the concern of all. The people came in large numbers, and in families – the little children, parents and grandparents all in church together; and the actual communion lasted long enough for three hymns to be sung during its course. All felt the service as their very own. A farmer milked his cows, delivered the milk, and then came two miles with his family on a motor cycle and side-car. A cowman rose at five o'clock to get his work done, another came with his wife who 'received the Blessed Sacrament with her baby in her arms and a little one of two years old by her side'. They all worshipped together in this way every Sunday. It taught them that they really were the Church, all alike in it and of it, an island of sanity and love in a frantic world; and that in the Church they walked with God for just so long as they walked together. When the service was over, they all had breakfast together (See "The Church of England from 1900-1965 by Roger Lloyd).*

Brother Edward was so sure that this Parish Communion was indeed a sign of the Church, the Body of Christ, working and worshipping as it should, that he strongly commended it as a key factor in his parish missions. For many of the churches he visited, the Parish Communion became a significant part of their renewal. In 1935, it was Brother Edward who inspired the liturgist Father Gabriel Hebert SSM to produce a book of essays entitled *The Parish Communion*. This book became a kind of manifesto for the movement to reform the Church's worship. It included Frank Fairbairn's description of the Temple Balsall Parish Communion and gave added impetus to the desire for change, which eventually led, via Series 2 and 3, to the Alternative Service Book of 1980 and the Common Worship prayer book authorised in 2000.

After his connection with Temple Balsall, Brother Edward continued his unflagging evangelistic work. He tried, not very successfully, to set up a religious community in Westcote in the Cotswolds. He succeeded in maintaining a network of evangelists who were prepared to work with him on parish missions in town and country. He never took a holiday, and deserves to be honoured as a godly and inspired servant of Christ, a true lover of Jesus, and one who never lost his burning desire to talk, preach and chat the Good News, especially among the poorer members of society and those whose faith in God was dim or virtually non-existent.

———<o>———

# The story of John Shirley

*I am indebted to John Burman F.R.Hist.S. who kindly gave his permission for me to re-tell this tale which was included in his book "In the Forest of Arden" (pub. Cornish Bros. Ltd 1948). I wonder how many residents of Shirley today are aware of how the name of the district they live in was 'donated' to a small boy in Madascar.*

The remarkable story of 'John Shirley' is worthy of a permanent record in print. It begins in 1869, when The Reverend Alfred Chiswell, a missionary in Madagascar, wrote to his friends in England in the following terms:

*We want to get hold of the little black boys and girls who scamper away from the Mission, crying out, "White man!" We want to bring them to live with us in our school so that they may learn about Him who said, "Suffer little children to come unto me." If my English friends will provide me with money to pay for food and clothing, I will take care that there shall be a place for them to live and be taught in. One child will cost three pounds and three shillings a year, so please let me ask some of my English friends to take some of the wild Malagasy children under their care, and I will undertake to send home full accounts of them and their progress.*

In response to this appeal, the Vicar of Shirley (The Revd. Charles Burd) asked for subscriptions from his parishioners, from a halfpenny to sixpence a month, and the response was satisfactory. In May of the following year, Mr Chiswell wrote to say that the boy adopted by the parish of Shirley was "purely heathen, purely ignorant, but shows some signs of intelligence." He was about twelve years old, a pure Malagasy and very black, with thick curly hair, and teeth like ivory. The boy's name was *Lavaloke*, meaning "long head", but when baptised, Mr Chiswell said, he would be given the name of John Shirley, and in time, he hoped that the boy might become a preacher or teacher among his own people. Finally, the missionary thanked the people of Shirley for what they were doing.

On 24 January 1872, Mr Chiswell made a favourable report on the boy, and we learn for the first time that he is a slave. The missionary also reported that the cost of living had increased, and that it would now cost four pounds and ten shillings a year to keep him. It is three years before we hear any more of him and then comes a letter from Mr (now Archdeacon) Chiswell, in which we first hear the black boy spoken of as John Shirley. The Archdeacon says (March 26^th 1877):

*John Shirley is now almost an historic name in our Mission. Several years ago I remember a very small boy, uncombed, unwashed, with scarcely a garment on him. When he came into our house he squatted in a distant corner, and scowled at me. You enabled me to clothe and feed him, and as time went on he changed most wonderfully. He was baptised. Now he is quite a young man, and a regular communicant. I am in hopes that eventually he may be of good service to the Church, in the way of teaching others at some Mission Station, but at present he is too young to have such a charge. What is more, his owner, who is a local District Governor, will shortly be replaced, and this will affect his movements. He speaks English very fairly indeed, and is the only boy I know in his position in life who has gained this knowledge, and he certainly has repaid the kindness your people have shown him.*

John Shirley wrote in his own language to the Vicar in the following February, and the translation was sent with the letter. The question of his freedom from slavery became urgent in October 1880. The cost was £30, and an appeal raised £70, part of it from St James Shirley, but there was delay in securing his freedom, for his old master had died. This news came in January 1882, and it was some years before anything more was heard of him. But his freedom from slavery was accomplished, and in 1888 he was ordained deacon, and the black slave boy became The Reverend John Shirley. In July of that year, Archdeacon Chiswell preached at St James' Church, and gave the news to the interested congregation. The following April the Vicar received a letter from John saying that he now had a wife and three daughters, and that his school had over a hundred pupils. He concluded with the words: "I visit the people of Shirley." He means in a spiritual sense, for he was never able to visit the people who rescued him from a 'heathen' existence. In 1905 a photograph of John Shirley was received in Shirley, but what became of it I do not know. He was then described as "a very gentle fellow; and has one of the sweetest voices I know. He is not a strong man. He is one of the quiet characters of whom there is not much to record." He had been ordained priest in 1895, and his name appears annually in Crockford's Clerical Directory, and for the last time in 1930, from which I assume that he died in that year, when he would have been about seventy-three.

—◄○►—

# Seasick to Nova Scotia
Solihull Parish News January 2013

Between 1917 and 1923 my father, The Revd. W. John Tunnicliffe served twice as a Chaplain in the Royal Navy, an experience that remained close to his heart throughout the rest of his life and ministry. His first posting was to HMS Cumberland (North American Station). This ship was an armoured cruiser of the Monmouth class, launched in 1904 and already obsolete by 1914. However, it was efficient enough to serve as escort to North Atlantic convoys between the United Kingdom and the U.S.A.

*We used to take gold to Nova Scotia and then go south to Chesapeake Bay to pick up a convoy to England. One Sunday we coaled ship and I was asked to help at the*

*Church of the Centurion at Old Point Comfort. It happened that President Wilson attended the 11.00 a.m. Eucharist, and I had to preach.*

Throwaway remarks like this in my father's fragmentary memoirs open up vistas for the imagination. How many Church of England clergy have preached to a congregation that contained the President of the United States of America?!

On HMS Cumberland my father found himself with a floating 'parish' of about 680 officers and men, which he served for 14 weeks to the "entire satisfaction" of the Captain (Captain's Certificate 22 Oct. 1917). The brevity of this posting may have been due to my father's being very prone to seasickness. Perhaps the Navy was showing compassion, or just simple common sense when, out of the subsequent six postings, five were mostly shore-based.

*I'm a poor sailor, so I was sent by the Chaplain of the Fleet to the Dover Patrol. I lived in the flagship, HMS Arrogant, which was tied up in Dover harbour. By invitation I used to go to sea in submarines or motor launches or destroyers, and my duties took me to Capel air station to minister to what became the Fleet Air Arm. Admiral Sir Roger Keyes was always kind and helpful. He and his band of heroes were the victors at Zeebrugge and Ostend. In my mess were fine men who had won the Victoria Cross.*

Details of this tour of duty from the archives of the Naval Chaplaincy Service read as follows:

- *Posted to the Dover Station for HMS Arrogant 22 September 1917 (special responsibility for submarines)*
- *Further Dover posting to HMS Arrogant 29 January 1918 (duty with Motor Launches of the 6$^{th}$ Flotilla in East Cliff also Coastal Motor Boats and Destroyers in the submarine harbour)*
- *Posted HMS Hecla 19$^{th}$ March 1919 for destroyers and attached vessels*
- *De-mobilised 24$^{th}$ April 1919.*

Certificates of Satisfaction for all these postings were given and carefully kept and remain among my father's papers. However satisfied my father and the Navy may have been with his work, he was prompted to leave the service for a while, possibly because of persistent seasickness, more likely because of the war's ending, and most likely because of his desire to marry my mother, Monica.

## The Zeebrugge Fiasco

When he joined the Navy in 1917, my father was still unmarried, and he was a postulant (novice monk) at The Community of the Resurrection in Mirfield. At the time this was his physical as well as his spiritual home. So he naturally wrote back "home" and his letters were printed in the Community's house magazine. This one makes fascinating reading, written just after the hopelessly unsuccessful attack on the German naval base at Zeebrugge.

### *H.M.S. "Arrogant" Dover.*

April 16th 1918

*We go on much as usual here… A few days ago a Captain of a submarine put his head into my cabin and said, "Padre, will you come and say a prayer for us before we go out?" And he went so far as to make arrangements for a Celebration in the submarine before they put to sea. But unfortunately he had to signal at the last minute to say that they could not manage it, as they had to go at short notice.[10] But it is cheering when these things come along. I noticed that this Captain came to the early Mass on the Sunday, and we had a long yarn together last night after dinner. As you know, these fellows are a fine lot, and if people only knew what they had to do they would understand what real sacrifices these men are called upon to make. Gradually I get to know people a little better – an officer here and a man there …. Easter Day was very cheering. Thanks to the Flag Captain we made the 9.30 a.m. service voluntary, and we had Holy Communion with hymns. The attendance was well up to the average, and 19 officers and about 24 men made their Communion …*

April 24th 1918 (the day after the Zeebrugge raid)

*At last the work for which preparations of a most exhaustive kind have been going on has been accomplished: and you will gather from the papers a good deal of what happened. But no account will be able to give in full all that the attack involved. We*

---

[10] This excursion would have been one of the several attempts that were made to attack Zeebrugge but had to be aborted on account of the weather conditions.

*have lost heavily, and men have gone from amongst us with whom it has been a grief to part. But all things considered, it is wonderful that we did not suffer more.*

*The submarine fellows did wonderfully. Four of a submarine crew were wounded by machine guns, which were trained on them at about fifty yards range, as soon as they started to pull away from the submarine which they abandoned. The Huns did not seem able to understand what the submarine was up to. They (the Huns) must have had her in full view by searchlight a mile before the submarine reached her destination. They may have thought that our fellows had lost their way, and that they (the Huns) would have an easy capture. In any case our fellows went right into the position which they were making for: and before they left the submarine they started the time fuse, which did its work when our crew was four hundred yards away. And five tons of amatol blew the viaduct (and the Huns thereon) into nothing. How some of our men came through it is difficult to understand: and a good deal of our work was carried out under very heavy fire. It was in one of these submarines that . . . x . . .[11] arranged for me to have a celebration before they set off: this, as I have said in my earlier letter, had to be abandoned. However, . . . x . . . came to Holy Communion on board here on the Sunday.*

*I went on board the "Vindictive" with our doctors when she got into harbour: and it was not difficult to imagine, from the evidence all round, what they had gone through. The Captain had four machine gun bullets through his cap, but escaped with a slight wound. When we got on board they were evacuating the wounded, and as we could not do anything to help we went on board a hospital yacht. There we left one of our doctors to assist in performing the operations which were going on. All day long officers and men kept on arriving on board here. Some had had to swim for life when they abandoned ship at Zeebrugge, and they were hungry and war-stained. We had a few hundred here at one time or another. I went back to the hospital yacht after lending an English Lieut-Commander a pair of flannel trousers and seeing him washed and fed and asleep on my bunk. The other padre had taken up his position aboard the yacht, so I came back and visited quarters to which men had returned. And now for some time visiting wounded, etc., and ships (viz., destroyers) will be the work ahead. Today I am burying a German sailor. He and two officers and four men were picked up after the disappearance of a U-boat some few days ago. Some day I may be able to give you a fuller account of what happened.*

---

[11]  The name was censored out of the letter.

That "fuller account" will have included a sad photograph, now in the Mirfield archives, of my father among a group of fellow-clergy, standing beside a mass grave in which are seen 66 coffins of Naval officers and men – victims from the Zeebrugge raid. One of the inevitable, less-welcome duties of a chaplain in the Armed Forces.

## Father Benson – a remarkable priest

Richard M. Benson was the founder of the Society of Saint John the Evangelist (more commonly known as The Cowley Fathers). He once made a brief stay in a large house in India. His host subsequently wrote: "Father Benson's influence in the house was extraordinary. When he had been living in the house for a week or so my servants, who could not speak English at all, came to me and said: 'What kind of holy man is this who has come to stay in the house? He never sleeps, but prays far into the hours of the night. He truly is a man of God.' When he left the house all the servants, Moslem and Hindu, lined up and made a profound salutation to him."

Father Benson was a spiritual leader of great stature and influence. He was once described as "one of the greatest spiritual forces in the English Church during the latter part of the 19th century." He was a contemplative and ascetic, yet a man of great energy and action. In 1866, while he was vicar of Cowley, he founded the first Anglican religious community for men, The Cowley Fathers, which within a short time was at work not only in Oxford but also in the USA, India and Africa. His theology of the Church and its mission was also astonishingly forward-looking, critical of his contemporary scene and surprisingly relevant to our own times. He was intensely sceptical of the triumphalism of the Christian missionary enterprise undertaken by the West in the wake of imperialism.

It was clear to Fr. Benson that any Christian action whatsoever had to derive from the basis of contemplative spirituality. At the Society's original home in Cowley, the chapel was on the top floor. Fr. Benson made good use of the symbolism of this location, in a remarkable piece of spiritual writing which is indicative of the deep devotional spring which formed the living source at the centre of his life and work.

*We come apart from the world to worship God. The children of Israel were called out of Egypt that they might go three days' journey into the wilderness to worship God. We are called out of the world into the wilderness of religion, in order that we may worship, in order that we may see God. God has appeared to us, and God wants us to come apart from the world in order that we may see Him. He desires to show Himself to us. He desires to make us experience the delight of His fellowship. He calls us apart for this express purpose . . . 'The Spirit and the Bride say, Come'. The Bride on earth, the Spirit with all the fullness of the utterance of God. We are called near to worship. The voice says 'Come up hither and I will show thee things which must be hereafter.' Oh! Whenever we come upstairs to our chapel let us think that we are coming up in obedience to that command. Let us expect to have the revelation of God. Let us remember that we are not coming up merely because we like to come, but because the voice has bidden us come. The bell as it tolls seems to speak these words, 'Come up hither and I will show thee things which must be hereafter.' Come up hither to say words which thou hast often said before, but come up hither to see a sight which thou hast not yet seen. Come up hither to do that which thou hast often done, but come up hither that I may do for thee that which thou hast not yet known. Our acts towards God are very limited, but God's revelation of Himself to the faithful worshipper is inexhaustible.*

***Tewkesbury Abbey***

Tewkesbury is best known for its battle (1471) and its abbey. That immediately puts me in mind of Battle Abbey near Hastings, wondering if battles and abbeys necessarily go together, considering that the former are the principal ingredient of war and the latter are erected in honour of the Prince of Peace. Yet if the Church is truly engaged in the battle against evil ... there's a sermon in there somewhere.

I dare say that the inhabitants of Tewkesbury bless the M5 for having relieved them of the heavy traffic that used to thunder through the middle of their town on the old A38. But those who whisk by on the motorway without a westward glance are missing a great architectural and spiritual treasure with a splendid musical tradition, not to mention the charm of the town itself.

As soon as you go inside the abbey, you are immediately aware of the extraordinary resonance of the building. Every sound echoes and re-echoes around for at least ten seconds. This makes it a challenging, yet exciting place in which to sing, as I discovered to my confusion on one occasion when I led my choir in sung Evensong there. In spite of our careful preparations, I pitched the leading reciting note incorrectly, and the mistake was mischievously caught and reverberated for all those seconds round the abbey to my chagrin and embarrassment and the amusement of the choir. The service, alas, was recorded for posterity, and I only hope that not too many folk still have the tape.

If you would like another smile relating to Tewkesbury Abbey, read the article *The Sermon* on page 48.

# CHAPTER TEN

# *Ouch!*

## Is God Fair?

Mike's Musings May 2007

"God does not leave the guilty unpunished; he punishes the children and their children for the sin of the parents to the third and fourth generation."                                                           Exodus 34.7

To our modern ears, this sounds like grossly unfair behaviour on the part of the Almighty. Why indeed should the children and grandchildren suffer for the sins of a previous generation? Before we attempt to find some explanation, let's not forget that The Bible is full of contradictions. So have a quick look at Ezekiel chapter 18 where you will find the opposite is robustly stated. The prophet is clearly in no doubt that each individual is totally responsible for their own actions.

Several points arise from this. The first is to note that the Bible in general has a tendency to overstate the case in order to make a point. Also, Biblical writers had far less difficulty than we do when it comes to dealing with apparent contradictions. They generally assume that the human mind is quite unable to comprehend the Supreme God who, in essence, is unknowable.

Another important point is to understand the diversity within the Bible and to allow for development in religious understanding. All Holy Scripture is, in a sense, under the inspiration of the Holy Spirit, "written for our learning" as Paul said (Romans 15.4). In another sense, the Bible covers the whole spectrum of the relationship between God and Man and is therefore inevitably full of apparent inconsistencies and different points of view.

Allowing for this, it is clear that the notion of the fathers' sins being visited upon the children comes from the idea of *collective responsibility for behaviour* which is a feature of the Divine Law as expounded in Exodus and Deuteronomy. This notion derives from the time when the Jewish religion was primarily tribal. In that kind of society, the cohesion of the tribe or clan is all-important, and the status and identity of the individual must be subordinated to the interests of the whole body. Under those circumstances, it is of paramount importance that a person should learn that if they step out of line and behave badly, that will have repercussions far beyond their immediate circle. That is a factor that is relevant to other societies and cultures, not least to our own. What kind of society, for example, are we preparing today for the next few generations, when family break-up is commonplace and global warming is causing biological mayhem?

**Prophetic utterance**

When we come to the time of Ezekiel, the context in the history of Israel is entirely different. Israel had long moved on from tribalism to nation-hood. Ezekiel's prophecy reflects a time when the nation had virtually been destroyed by Babylon, and a demoralised remnant of it was in exile. At such a time of disintegration, it was important for the people to learn about individual, rather than collective, responsibility, especially when it came to dealing with the timeline, past and future. Clearly, God has new plans for his people (see Isaiah, chapters 40-55), and it is of little use for them to dwell, at this stage, on the effects of wrong actions from the past or into the future. They need to see how each and every one of them is totally accountable to God in the present, for their world has changed – the past is destroyed and the future is precarious.

Once again though, this prophetic teaching in Ezekiel 18 seems to relate to other ages and circumstances including our own. We are now dealing with matters of sin and responsibility. The Abrahamic religions, Judaism, Christianity and Islam, are all in broad agreement that human beings are endowed by God with a sense of responsibility and freedom of choice. Therefore sin must be taken seriously, and dealt with one way or another. Part of the task of religion is to develop the conscience and encourage a sense of moral responsibility. People sometimes try to explain bad behaviour by saying "it's all in the genes." This is the latest in a series of strategies whereby modern human beings have looked for ways of avoiding moral responsibility or ways of making excuses for sin. Other strategies have used other words, such as "free", "evolution", "possessed", "neurosis", or even "my star sign".

Using prayers of confession, privately or in our church services, is a spiritually healthy reminder that we are responsible for our own sins.

Is God fair? The short answer is "Yes, always". He is also compassion-ate and forgiving. But that need not prevent us from continuing to engage with questions about determinism and freewill, nature and nurture. These will continue to tease the human mind for as long as there are people prepared to think and to argue about them, and I suspect that they will not be resolved this side of heaven!

# Why did God make wasps?
Solihull Parish News July/August 2019

The question was articulated in clear treble tones on number one platform at Moor Street Station when I was waiting for the train. That must have been at least ten years ago, and I haven't stopped thinking about it since. Sadly, my train came in before I got to hear the parent's reply, a response that might have given me a handle on to the theology of this teasing question.

Over the years I have tended to echo the child's question quite often, especially when wasps got into the bathroom, a place where you emphatically don't want them! In five simple words, it opens up what is possibly the most difficult and longstanding theological debate that the human race has entered into over centuries of religious discourse. You might call it simply "the nuisance factor", but there is a wide spectrum of setbacks that afflict us. At the lower end are the normally not-too-serious nuisances like wasps; at the other end is the serious and inescapable problem of evil and suffering. This is when we look at the dread cocktail of natural disaster and human wickedness and ask the question 'Why?' As if that in itself was not difficult enough to understand, we make it still more complicated by professing a faith in a God who is good: a God who is Love.

The honest answer to the conundrum has to be "I don't know." Beware of anyone who comes up with a simple, ready-made solution. Yet there are pointers that can help as we think and debate, one of which is the question of pain. It is natural for us to avoid pain, and to find ways of alleviating it. Yet in medicine, pain is often an essential signal that something else is wrong, so that if you simply take a painkiller you could be masking the problem and thus do yourself more harm.

Now widen your perspective. Youth violence and knife-crime are clearly evil. So the public clamours for more resourcing for the police, for the criminal justice system and for prisons. Yet funding is sadly lacking for social work among young people and for research into the causes of violence. As with medicine, it is of little use dealing with the symptoms without tackling the causes.

## The wider picture

It is only by widening our perspective that we can begin to make some sense of a God-filled universe that contains within it elements of suffering and evil. The disciplines of Science and Art can often help us.

Science is sometimes regarded as the enemy of religion. It is nothing of the sort! Like all human endeavour, Science can make mistakes. It has put a foot wrong by bringing us to the point where we expect the world to be ordered for our personal benefit and comfort. Also Science has often falsely claimed that it alone has the answer to all human problems, and that nothing is real that cannot be observed and measured by human beings.

On the other hand, Science has opened up for us the stupendous mystery of the universe, from the sub-atomic to the mega-galactic. Importantly for us now, it is teaching us to think and act globally, which is a vital necessity at every level. So we can partially answer the child's question by our knowledge that wasps are part of an intricate and delicate eco-system upon which our very existence on this planet depends.

What about Art? I recently wrote an article suggesting that we might consider God as a mathematician. To think of God as an artist is, to my mind, even more helpful. Look closely at a work of art. As likely as not you will see that it consists of a collection of ugly daubs and smears and scratches totally unpleasing to the eye. Stand back, and you see a masterpiece. It is a question of your perspective, your viewpoint.

Alert, sensitive, intelligent human beings will continue to wrestle with the problem of evil. The question "Why?" will never (perhaps should never) be met with a self-assured "Because …" My own viewpoint is that, in this life, human beings can only be aware of a fragment of Reality, a fragment that is appropriate to us at this stage in our existence. True scientists, true artists and true saints get a clearer glimpse than most of us of the spiritual Reality that surrounds us on every side and at every level. Haltingly, but sometimes beautifully, they can share their vision with the rest of us. But it is only faith and trust in God, who is Love, that can help us to find meaning and purpose in life when we are up against hard questions concerning evil and suffering.

# The problem of pain
## Mikes Musings April 2007

Here's an interesting comment on the subject from Dan Brown, the author of "The Da Vinci Code". This argument about why God should allow suffering comes in a conversation between the Papal Chamberlain (the Camerlengo) and a lieutenant of the Vatican Swiss guard called Chartrand. The novel by Dan Brown is called "Angels and Demons" which is an extravagant fantasy, but not a bad read for all that. The Camerlengo starts the dialogue:

Camerlengo: You are confused because the Bible describes God as an omnipotent and benevolent deity.

Chartrand: Exactly.

Camerlengo: Omnipotent-benevolent simply means that God is all-powerful *and* well-meaning.

Chartrand: I understand the concept. It's just ... there seems to be a contradiction.

Camerlengo: Yes. The contradiction is pain. Man's starvation, war, sickness ...

Chartrand: Exactly! ... Terrible things happen in this world. Human tragedy seems like proof that God could not possibly be *both* all-powerful and well-meaning. If He *loves* us and has the *power* to change our situation, He would prevent our pain, wouldn't He?

Camerlengo: 'Would He?

*Chartrand felt uneasy. Had he overstepped his bounds? Was this one of those religious questions you just didn't ask?*

Chartrand: Well ... if God loves us, and He can protect us, he would *have* to. It seems He is either omnipotent and uncaring, or benevolent and powerless to help.

Camerlengo: Do you have children, Lieutenant?

Chartrand: No, signore.

Camerlengo: Imagine you had an eight-year-old son ... would you love him?

Chartrand:      Of course.

Camerlengo:      Would you do everything in your power to prevent pain in his life?

Chartrand:      Of course.

Camerlengo:      Would you let him skateboard?

Chartrand:      Sure, I'd let him skateboard, but I'd tell him to be careful.

Camerlengo:      So as this child's father, you would give him some basic, good advice and then let him go off and make his own mistakes?

Chatrand:      I wouldn't run behind him and mollycoddle him if that's what you mean.

Camerlengo:      But what if he fell and skinned his knee?

Chartrand:      He would learn to be more careful.

Camerlengo:      So although you have the *power* to interfere and prevent
(smiling)      your child's pain, you would *choose* to show your love by letting him learn his own lessons?

Chartrand:      Of course. Pain is part of growing up. It's how we learn.

*The Camerlengo nodded.*   Exactly.

———◁○▷———

# The unpalatable truth
### Solihull Parish Magazine January 2016

What on earth can you do when terrorists and suicide bombers let loose murder and mayhem? The immediate responses in Western society are, first, deep shock, outrage and horror accompanied by a feeling almost of numb despair. After that comes the outpouring of grief, sympathy and support for the sufferers, together with heart-warming assurances of solidarity.

This initial response is closely followed by two very predictable, but far more questionable, reactions. First there is the overwhelming media attention. While this does inform us of what has happened, it also tends to feed the seemingly unending Western appetite for sensation and the macabre. Then comes the dread side-effect: the media provide instant free publicity for the terrorists and their masters. Along with this comes the struggle of the politicians to find an appropriate reaction. Their rhetoric inevitably centres on retribution, punishment of offenders, and destruction of the radical movement and its followers who are perceived to be the cause of the terrorist activities. This often implies military intervention and bombardment.

So much for the purely secular repercussion. What about the response of the Christian Church? Have we anything to offer beyond our truly heartfelt abhorrence of terrorism and our deep empathy and prayer-support for the innocent victims? How do we deal with the question we so much dread: where is God in all this?

I fear that the real answers to this line of questioning are too often ones that we shy away from, because they convey an unpalatable truth. Far from being absent, tucked away in some remote heavenly dwelling and blandly indifferent, God is intimately engaged in his creation at every point. He ... (excuse me if I use the male pronoun: I think of God as 'He/She' but this is clumsy in print) ... God is as much in the blood, sweat, toil and anguish which characterises the perpetual struggle for survival and development, as He is in the glory and splendour of the micro- and macro- cosmos. In recent times, the Christian Church in the West has been so absorbed in polishing up its image and trying to increase its membership that it has almost totally forgotten its *prophetic* role and responsibility. Our Bible is full of calamities, whether as a result of natural events like floods and famines, or as a direct consequence of human nastiness like oppression, war and terrorism. There are a few instances (in the Psalms for example) where a lone voice cries out to God, "why is this happening: where are you?" But the main thrust of Scripture in its dealing with calamity puts God right in the foreground, and highlights the Prophets as God's spokesmen.

The prophetic messages are very clear, and most of them are unpalatable. They do not say "the enemy is to blame". The Prophets proclaim in strident terms, "You, God's people, have got it wrong." And the remedy is always the same: not a knee-jerk reaction to increase the cycle of violence, but a call to the nation for deep self-appraisal, humble confession, and repentance. You don't have to leaf through many pages of the Bible to hear that prophetic message: but when did you last hear it proclaimed in a church sermon, or read it in a church magazine, or listen to it in a pronouncement from a Christian leader?

## The prayer of Daniel

In the wake of one of the terrorist atrocities of 2015, I found myself profoundly moved while reading the 9th chapter of the Book of Daniel in the Old Testament. The book was written during the Maccabean period of Jewish history, about 160 years before the time of Christ. This was a time of cruel oppression and strife. Daniel's heartfelt prayer echoes the familiar prophetic voice from previous generations. When I read it, I found myself returning to the Prayer of Confession in the 1662 Book of Common Prayer.

At a time of pain, fear and anxiety, when people are asking "Where is God in all this?" it is tempting to try and find a suitable religious catch phrase which can only be superficial, or just to slink away in confusion. I find it more useful, even though it is uncomfortable, to recite carefully and reflectively: "*We have* erred … *we have* strayed from thy ways like lost sheep … *We have* followed *too much* the devices, and desires, of *our own* hearts …" and so on.

Some people reckon that the 1662 Prayer Book liturgy is over-weighted with reminders of sin and calls to repentance. It is as well to remember that it was first published just after England had emerged from the terrors and mayhem of civil war with all its brutality, including the beheading of a king, much of it carried out in the name of religion. The common rhetoric in our generation is that Western civilization has got it right and the terrorists have got it wrong. I think we need a more balanced look at our own history. We also need a much more careful appraisal of who is currently absorbing most of the earth's resources, who is manufacturing most of the world's armaments, and who is contriving to increase, rather than to reduce, the gap between the haves and the have-nots.

However unpalatable and unpopular the prophetic truths in the Bible may be, it is clearly the Church's task to proclaim them as best we can to our own generation. If *we* don't do it, no one else will.

**All Saints Church, Shard End**

This is the 'centre' for the encircling parish of Shard End (see the next article, "Circles without Centres"). It is the first major post-World War II church to be built in the diocese of Birmingham. It was consecrated on November 1st, All Saints Day, in 1955. The architect was John Osborne. Two days after its consecration, Her Majesty Queen Elizabeth II accompanied by Prince Philip visited the church and placed their royal signatures in the Visitors' Book.

The tower is much more imposing than it appears in my sketch. The Shard End housing estate was planned by the city of Birmingham during the 1930s. The planners had an eye to garden cities such as Welwyn in Hertfordshire. The original drawings of the Shard End estate show broad tree-lined avenues, and a sweeping vista along the principal highway from the city leading to a prestigious and prominent parish church.

Alas! The post-war pressure on housing severely distorted their vision. In some areas, instead of the standard two-storey dwellings, four-storey houses-upon-houses were constructed. Many of the intended open spaces were built on, and eventually those horrors of the 1960s, multi-storey tower blocks, made their appearance. The planners then saw fit to obliterate All Saints church from view by partially surrounding it with shops and flats.

# CHAPTER ELEVEN

# *You*

## Circles without Centres
### Solihull Parish Magazine April 2010

During the early nineteen fifties, the Bishop of Birmingham, Leonard Wilson, placed a big wooden cross on a patch of bare ground close to Castle Bromwich. He considered that he was marking the centre of a large circle. In that spot today stands the parish church of All Saints Shard End, which the Bishop consecrated in 1955.

When he came to the diocese, Bishop Wilson soon became aware of the vast expansion of housing estates around the city. He called these new suburbs *Circles Without Centres*, and that phrase became the catchy title for the initiative to build new churches. The encircling suburbs needed spiritual centres, and All Saints was the first to be built.

The bishop's initiative was bold, but it was not innovative: for it stood in a tradition that reached back at least to Saint Augustine of Canterbury in the sixth century, a tradition of Christianising Britain. Preaching crosses were set up before any churches were built. The objective was always the same: to create centres of spiritual excellence that would influence the locality where they were put, and the people who lived there.

Today, many suburban churches are struggling to keep their heads above the inflowing waters of agnosticism, secularism and atheism, if not hostility. Under these conditions, there is a great temptation for a church to become the opposite of what it should be, in other words, to become a kind of **centre** without a **circle**. Christians tend to gather together for mutual support and comfort, feeling lost in a sea of indifference, and apparently having no Christian influence beyond that which they minister to one another. Today, at All Saints, and many other churches up and down the country, a building large enough to hold 400 worshippers is being kept precariously afloat by a faithful handful of about 20 members. Even in churches that are well supported, the temptation to become a centre without a circle is always there. For it is much easier to belong to a social club for mutual support and comfort than to be a part of a living organism that reflects the glory of God in a God-lacking society.

## Individuals

Reflecting on circles and centres, I began to realise that individuals also can easily become centres without circles. I have a close relative who seldom gets in touch with me. When I go to see him, I find that he and his small family have more or less lost the art of conversation. At any time, our talk may be interrupted by the mobile phones which take precedence in their house. They appear to have an astonishing lack of interest in anything beyond the small circle of themselves and their close buddies.

But let's not become too judgmental. When you come to think about it, each one of us is the centre of a sphere of influence. How we think and how we behave has an effect on other people, for good or ill. When things get tough for us, we have a tendency to turn in on ourselves and become self-centred, even selfish: to become a centre without a circle. That is bad news, both for us and for other people. A Christian is a person who is challenged by Jesus to recognise this tendency and to do something about it. If we really are trying to be as God would have us be, then we need to be rigorously honest with ourselves, keeping ourselves under review but without being morbid about it. Praying the prayer of confession from time to time (not just in church) can help. "Yes, Lord: I *have* erred, and strayed like a lost sheep. I have followed too much the devices and desires of my own heart" (I prefer the old words).

With a bit of honest self-appraisal and God's help, we can turn from being self-absorbed to become a centre of spiritual excellence. In so doing, we become what we were meant to be in the first place, centres with circles of influence, which is precisely what the saints and missionaries have been throughout the ages.

Forty-four years ago I met a man in Shard End called Dennis. He was totally paralysed, and spent the final twelve years of his life in bed. He was confirmed by the Bishop who came to his bedside for the ceremony, and after that he regularly received the Sacrament of Holy Communion. He was a person of great faith and great simplicity. He was one of the blest "pure in heart". Dennis had an extraordinary influence. People visited him constantly. Often these were troubled people, and they always went away from Dennis feeling better. He was uncomplicated, unsophisticated, un-famous and ordinary. At his funeral, the church was full. He was, I think, one of the most un-self-centred people I have met, somehow the centre of a circle of goodness that derived from him.

—◦—

# Are you talented? (Matthew 25. 14-30)
### Solihull Parish Magazine February 2006

I find it helpful to compare the means by which Jesus communicated his message with that of the modern cartoonist. There is deliberate, careful, and sometimes witty exaggeration in order to make the point. Not that the message loses any of its seriousness, just as some cartoons are very serious in intent. The parables are carefully crafted, stylistically, as cartoons are carefully drawn. They were crafted by Jesus in the first place, and then each evangelist re-worked them according to their own way of writing and to meet most effectively the needs of the particular congregation for whom they were written and to whom they were read.

Some of the parables of Jesus, by no means all, end up like the well-known Parable of the Talents, with wailing and gnashing of teeth. This kind of stylistic cadence was popular with Matthew, and one wonders whether he didn't perhaps overdo it a bit. Maybe his congregation (possibly Syrian and largely Jewish) either liked that kind of approach, or needed it to jolt them a bit. Be that as it may, the parable is skilfully narrated, and makes its point effectively, not just for its first audiences, but also for any subsequent reader, including ourselves.

You will recall the storyline. Three employees are given a certain amount of money by their boss who is off on a business trip. They are expected to imitate the boss and use the money creatively to enhance his business enterprise. The first two do just that, and they are commended for their initiative by the boss on his return, and duly rewarded. The third chap decides to avoid any risk, to save his energy, and simply return the cash he was entrusted with. His end is a touch sticky, Matthew's "wailing and gnashing of teeth."

There was plenty of wailing and gnashing of teeth going on in the world that the early Christians faced, and in that respect the world has not changed. Violence and evil deeds remain an uncomfortable part of the scene, and human beings appear unable to learn from past mistakes. Perpetrators and victims alike can be caught up in this inability, or reluctance (which is it?) to find a way through. For instance, every time we call for vengeance and punishment without any constructive thought about the causes of the malaise that fuel human aggression, then we are siding with the enemy, and will only add to the wailing and teeth-gnashing. In this connection, the Parable of the Talents has a useful message to convey to people of any generation.

## What is your talent?

The word "talent" has a double meaning. In the ancient world, it was a large sum of money, deriving from the idea of weight and worth. For us, it is an endowment, a gift that we are given at birth. The original hearers of the parable would have realised that Jesus was not talking about money, and it is because of the story that our modern use of the word emerged when the Bible was translated into English in the late Middle Ages.

The first two servants in the story are commended, because they recognise the potential of the talents they were entrusted with. They could increase in value, be productive and useful. "Look master," they said, "we have increased the value of the talents you entrusted us with." But the spotlight falls most revealingly on the third servant. He could only summon up sufficient energy and enterprise to *bury* his talent, and ultimately return it to the Lord unchanged.

It is often assumed that talents are confined to clever people who have a particular expertise. If you think that way, you are not going to get the point of this story. The truth is that each one of us has been given talents, which, too often, we simply bury and hide. As human beings made in God's image, we have talents for goodness, for creative kindness, for generosity, for understanding and self-sacrifice. There is no doubt that these are the very attributes that are the most effective antidotes against human badness, destructive aggression, ignorance and selfishness.

You simply cannot defeat badness and violence with more badness and violence, for each feeds on the other and the situation can only worsen. When will that lesson be learnt, especially by those in authority? Evil, in the form of greed, corruption and violent behaviour, can only be overcome by the good talents that I have just mentioned. So if the badness in the world and in society seems to be increasing, it is because the talents of goodness lie buried and unused.

This is an axiom that applies on the small scale in the home and family, and the familiar social groupings to which we all belong. It also applies, I believe, to the nation as a whole. In his inaugural sermon (2005), the Archbishop of York included a rallying call to the English church and nation. Although we Brits are by no means angelic, we do have certain attributes that are worth mentioning, not least because they have often been recognised by people beyond our shores. We are quite good at the art of diplomacy and finding compromises when situations become confrontational. Connected with this talent for tolerance are other British characteristics, such as a gift for dogged perseverance when things get really tough (World Wars 1 and 11), and gifts of resilience, inventiveness, and a common-sense approach to life and its problems.

**Fragility**

In all this, though, we need to be very much aware of the fragility in modern society of these important talents. They can be so easily buried under a heap of polarised and partisan thinking, which can sometimes verge on arrogant extremism. In a similar way, our native talent for what we call "fair play" is being buried under a pile of greed and fraudulent practise. Our talent for forbearance and making-the-best-of-a-bad-job is under threat of being buried beneath a mound of litigation. And our talent for common sense is rapidly disappearing under an unsavoury heap of political correctness and bureaucracy.

Every threat, however, is also a challenge, not just to those who lead and teach and make policies, but also to ordinary people. We really need to recognise and dig up and re-assert those talents for reasonableness and for making good relationships that we know we have but sometimes lose sight of. The way to do this is, first of all, to renew our thanksgiving to God for the goodness of the gifts he has given us. Then, to use those gifts for the benefit of other people, and to tell others about them, especially our young people. We are led to believe (often by the media) that a doomwatch scenario prevails. In fact, this is not true. Rogues and extremists and the morally corrupt are a distinct minority in the world. But we do need to realise that this evil minority will cause far more wailing and teeth-gnashing if we hide and bury our God-given talents instead of flaunting them and putting them to good and profitable use.

The parable, therefore, has relevance for today. When Jesus first spoke it, there was a distinct sense of urgency in his teaching. There was already wailing and gnashing of teeth, and he could see more to come. The same is true for us. So let's get our shovels out, and dig up those buried talents before it's too late.

◦

# My Baptism
### Solihull Parish Magazine July 2010

There is a story that when the devil came to tempt Martin Luther, the scholar threw his inkwell at him and said very loudly in Latin: "I am baptised!" True or not, the story reminds us to place a high value on our baptism. Have another look at the story of the baptism of Jesus by his cousin John in the River Jordan (Mark 1 verses 9 – 11 and paralleled in the other Gospels). It raises an interesting point about the relationship between religious ritual and spiritual experience, and also about God's timing.

Jesus waited thirty years before his baptism. When it happened, the event was accompanied by a profound spiritual experience. There was an opening of the heavens and the descent of the Spirit of God in the form of a dove. What began as a religious ritual of purification became, for Jesus, a decisive moment of divine revelation and choice. There are a great many people, some of whom call themselves "born-again Christians", who think that the authentic life of the spirit depends on tangible spiritual and emotional experiences. Such people often hold the opinion that the faithful performance of religious ritual in prayer and common worship are inauthentic and unnecessary. Nothing could be further from the truth. The Bible, the life and witness of Jesus, and the wisdom of the great religions of the world all affirm this. To put it bluntly, you cannot be a Christian in the fullest sense without going to church.

During his travels, Saint Paul arrived at Ephesus. There he discovered a group of disciples of John the Baptist who were transferring their allegiance to Jesus (see Acts 19 verses 1-7). When Paul questioned them about their religious initiation he found that they had, as Luke put it, "received John's baptism." This raises all sorts of questions about the Baptist movement in the first century, which you can read about in scholarly books.

Paul would have told these new believers that the new, Spirit-filled, reign of God on earth was now beginning because of Jesus, with John as the herald of the good news. Because of Jesus, people were being invited to connect with God in a new and different way. Faith in Jesus would mean that the Holy Spirit would empower people to discover new things about God, and help them to look at the world in a new light, to see that the world was both God-filled and God-loved. So these 'John Baptist' disciples in Ephesus were baptised in the name of Jesus Christ. Just like Jesus at his baptism, they experienced at their re-birth the touch of God. For them, the religious ritual and the spiritual experience coincided. With Saint Paul, you will remember, it was the other way round.

## Timing

What about us? Our religious rituals, whether baptism, confirmation, prayer, or any other form of worship, may or may not be attended by a spiritual experience. It does not matter, for God has his own timing for these things. I expect that many of you, like me, will have had such an experience at some time or another: one of those heightened moments when God gave us a nudge in his direction and away from our own self-centred concerns. For myself, I was born on 3 August 1931, and on 2 September 1931 I was born again by water and the Spirit at my baptism. I don't actually recall either of these momentous events. When I was confirmed I didn't have a religious experience like the Christians of Ephesus; neither, probably, did you. But we did all receive the gift of God's Holy Spirit at our baptism and again at our confir-mation, even if this gift remained dormant within us for years. That is why it is a good thing, from time to time, to check up on the dates of your baptism and remember them as an anniversary. We celebrate birth-days, so why not rebirth-days?

God's timing is not the same as ours, and the baptism of Jesus is a case in point. We know virtually nothing about Jesus before his baptism, which took place about thirty years after he was born. That seems like a waste of time; but not so in God's timing. When the right time comes, and God gives us a nudge, whether before, during, or after our baptism, then we must be ready to respond. We shall be able to do this more readily if we bear in mind three factors that relate to life as a Christian:

# CALLING   COLLECTIVITY   COST

CALLING    At his baptism Jesus heard unmistakably the call of God: *You are my beloved*. We were also called by God at our baptism, even if we were unaware at the time. We received our vocation, an invitation into the life of Christ, a calling to follow him. This was an invitation once and for all, yet constantly it is renewed: *Come to me: follow me*. It is an invitation to explore God and, with his help, to view the world and our life in the world in new and different ways. As followers of Christ, we should be critical, perhaps unconventional and non-conformist as Jesus was, with respect to the prevailing values and attitudes of a decadent society. That is our *Calling*.

COLLECTIVITY    The baptism of Jesus in the river Jordan was not a private, but a very public affair, in company with hundreds of others. We know that immediately after it, Jesus spent time on his own, but his life and ministry were very much a corporate and collective experience among a group of friends, and among crowds of people. So, too, our baptism was in a company: certainly among family and friends, but attended by that "cloud of witnesses" referred to in Hebrews 12, saints and angels and fellow-Christians of all generations were there, unseen witnesses, at our baptism. Our spiritual life may have its solitary times, but it is necessarily pursued *Collectively*, in company with the faithful, whether few or many. We are called to support one another in the faith, not just to plough a lonely furrow.

COST    The *Cost* of discipleship is a common theme, but it is rather easy to set it aside when one is comfortable. There is no need to be gloomy about it: the Christian life is characterised by joy, the joy of believing, and the joy of our relationship with God, with Jesus, and with one another in the fellowship of the Holy Spirit. But we do live in a real world. In the life of the spirit we are surrounded by the "cloud of witnesses", but in the life of the world we are surrounded by unbelievers, many of whom mock our faith, and some of whom attack and despise it. Our baptism means that we are signed up to a disciplined approach to life of which the prime elements are high standards and self-control. Being baptised as a Christian is not a cheap option.

So it doesn't matter very much whether or not we remember our baptism, whether or not we have holy feelings in church or while we are praying, whether or not we feel uplifted or cast down, or just neutral as we do our best to lead the Christian life. What matters is that we *are* baptised and that we are constantly washed and cleansed by God because of Jesus., Because of baptism, it matters that we have received the gift of God's Spirit and that we are part of a great company, a collection of faithful people who have heard and accepted God's call and have responded to it down the centuries.

⎯⎯⎯⎯◆⎯⎯⎯⎯

# Being a Rep
### Solihull Parish Magazine May 2017

I was listening on the radio to the uplifting setting of the *Benedictus* by Karl Jenkins from his celebrated Mass for Peace. I can remember just sufficient school Latin to understand the words, and they came across to me with a new sense of urgency: *Benedictus qui venit in nomine Domini* ... Blessed is the one who comes in the name of the Lord. Suddenly, and unexpectedly, those words applied to me!

I realised with a new clarity that, as a Christian, wherever I may go, I go 'in the name of the Lord'. Or perhaps the meaning is that whenever I arrive in a different place, I should be mindful that I arrive in the name of the Lord. Even if I am about my own business, I don't cease to be a Christian, i.e. a representative of the Lord Jesus. I cannot blot out my baptism.

Now honesty compels me to say that, in practical day-to-day life and affairs, this is often, perhaps usually, far from the case. When I am about my own business, my Christian heritage and calling is usually far from the front of my mind. When I am pursuing my own agenda, whether public or private, I frequently set aside the ideals of Christianity and the teachings of the Gospel. In the language of the Book of Common Prayer, I err, and stray from God's ways like a lost sheep. That way, I miss out on blessings. Because the Benedictus reminds us quite forcefully that when we come to *wherever*, or meet with *whoever* 'in the name of the Lord' then there will be blessings: *blessed is the one who comes in the name of the Lord.* And without doubt that blessedness will spill over into the environment and among the people with whom we are engaging.

When I left university I worked for a while as a sales representative for a well-known and respected company. The first approach to a potential customer was always along the line of, "My name is Martin Tunnicliffe and I am representing Messrs. ……….. Ltd. My identity, however significant in its own right, was inseparable from that of the firm. This is a fair analogy for any Christian. Our identity is affirmed when we are named at our baptism, but we are baptised "in the name of" God the Trinity, Father, Son and Holy Spirit. If we sign up to that commitment, whether at baptism or confirmation, then wherever we go in the world, we are actually representatives for Jesus. An awesome thought!

I think, however, that we shouldn't press the analogy too far. Unless we are actively called to engage in evangelism, we don't, and shouldn't, as a rule, greet people by saying, "Hello, I am representing Jesus." Nevertheless, I am sure that in our everyday encounters, we could, as Christians, be more mindful that we are in fact the Lord's representatives in the world. And that means accepting the demands that the Gospel makes on believers, along with the great blessings that faith can bring. The more we can joyfully live the Benedictus, the more cause there will be for others joyfully to shout or sing 'Hosanna!'

# CHAPTER TWELVE

# *The Lord's Prayer*

## Daily Bread 1

*looking below the surface of The Lord's Prayer*

Solihull Parish Magazine December 2013

This article begins in the supermarket while the weekly shopping was sliding towards my end of the checkout. There I was at my task, stowing the various items in the bags and hefting them into the waiting trolley. Recently during this operation, I suddenly found myself saying, "Give us this day our daily bread." How many hundreds, perhaps thousands, of times have I repeated those words. But now they begin to disturb me. I am asking myself: what do they really mean? More than that, I am asking: what do they imply?

When I got home, after stowing away the generous contents of the car boot, I dusted off the one scholarly book that I have on The Lord's Prayer *(The Lord's Prayer by Ernst Lohmeyer: Collins 1965)*. In his introduction the author reminded me of an important fact about the prayer: *Everyone can understand it, yet it always calls for a new understanding.* I then went on to read again the chapter about this particular petition. Like the prayer as a whole, it sounds simple and obvious. In child's language it seems to be saying *Please God, give me enough to eat today.* But even this re-statement already elaborates the petition: we have interpreted the word 'bread' as meaning 'food.' That is perfectly legitimate: the Bible does it just like we do. The Hebrew word *lehem* (*lahma* in Aramaic) describes not only what is baked from wheat flour but any food whatsoever; in particular the phrase *eat bread* simply means *have a meal* (Genesis 28.20; Exodus 16.15; Deuteronomy 10.18; Isaiah 55.10 and lots more. In fact, in modern Bibles, when the translators come across the Hebrew and Greek words for *bread,* they often translate it as *food).* It also seems reasonable to extend the meaning of *daily bread* to include other basic necessities for decent living such as shelter, clothing etc.

What about the words *today* and *daily*? This is where the petition starts to get both difficult and challenging. The challenge came to me at the supermarket, seeing the trolley loaded with enough for at least a week, perhaps longer. When I got back home I glanced at the larder, briefly considered the contents of the rest of the house, and finally the bank balance, and I began to wonder what I am up to when I pray "Give us *today* (or as Luke's Gospel says "give us *day by day*") our *daily* bread". There's no doubt about it: I am challenged. Here is a clear limiting factor in the world's most famous prayer for sustenance, almost a directive to live each day as it comes, but I am mightily concerned about security and the future.

We live in a world in which poverty and even destitution are the norm for the majority. I expect that you, like me, are blessed with a good deal more than the simple basic necessities of life. That being the case, we need to face up squarely to the challenge that is implied in The Lord's Prayer. Consumerism is contrary to the teaching of the Bible, especially the teaching of Jesus (see Matthew 6. 31-34).

## Generosity

This petition about daily bread stands at the very centre of the Christians' most treasured and most used prayer. In the first place, it relates intimately to the clear teaching of both the Old and the New Testaments about the abundance of God's generosity in providing what is needful for his children (Psalms 107.9 & 146.7; Proverbs 30.8; Luke 1.53; James 1.17). Secondly, it connects with the requirement that we, God's family, must reflect his generosity by sharing the abundance of his gifts (Isaiah 58.7; James 2.15-16; 1 John 3.17).

So this petition is about lifestyle as much as it is about adequate nourishment. A very common human fault is to acquire, and to hold on to, more than we need for the present, just in case. Praying The Lord's Prayer, we are constantly reminded that we must balance prudence with active compassion towards those in need, and also with common sense, i.e. we might die tomorrow (see Luke 12. 13-20).

I reckon that it is far more difficult for us to be sincere in praying "give us this day our daily bread" than it was for most of the first-century followers of Jesus. This is simply because most of them were living at what we would describe as a third-world level: they were non-affluent, subject to constant food shortages due to climate or politics, and existing under precarious health conditions with a life expectancy of around forty years. Praying for sufficient food to meet the needs of the next 24 hours is a heartfelt plea for someone who is not sure where the next meal is coming from. I doubt if anyone reading this is in that situation any more than I am.

My take on this petition then, especially when I am in the supermarket, is to pray that our affluent society may somehow learn (using a phrase borrowed from Christian Aid) to "live more simply so that others may simply live." And it seems apt to continue at that point with the next phrase, "forgive us our trespasses." Try it next time you go shopping.

There is still more to be learnt from this *daily bread* petition. The very word "daily" is a conundrum. The Greek word is *epiousios*, and my scholarly guide says that, from the second century onward, "a small library has been written about this word ... but its riddle has only partially been solved, and that with no degree of certainty." Also, there are subtle reasons why Jesus used the plural form, *us* and *our* which need looking into. It seems that another article may be called for, so (as they say) "watch this space."

—————◦—————

# Daily Bread 2
Solihull Parish Magazine January 2014

On the Mount of Olives, just outside Jerusalem, stands the Church of the Paternoster. There has been a church on this site since the early centuries of Christianity. A nearby cave is traditionally thought to be the place where Jesus gave teaching to his disciples, specifically The Lord's Prayer. Around the cloister is a series of coloured tiles depicting The Lord's Prayer in 140 different languages including Aramaic, the language that Jesus and his disciples would have normally spoken.

The Gospels of Matthew and Luke, in which The Lord's Prayer appears, were written in Greek. The English words that we use for the prayer are translated from the Greek text. The first-century Aramaic that Jesus spoke is now a 'dead' language, but by a careful study of ancient texts, linguistic and biblical scholars have been able to re-create it and write The Lord's Prayer in Aramaic. However, there is one word that poses a problem. In English that word is 'daily', the adjective used in the petition 'give us this day our daily bread.' As I mentioned in the previous article, in the Greek text the word is *epiousios*. And the problem is that this word does not appear in any other Greek text.[12] Scholars have been able to find Aramaic words that are equivalent to all the other Greek words of The Lord's Prayer, except *epiousios*.

What, then, does a translator do when he comes across a word that is unique in the original language, a word of which nobody knows the meaning? The answer has to be 'intelligent guesswork'. Many pints of scholarly ink have been used by experts in biblical studies trying to resolve this conundrum. Their several arguments are too complex to deal with in a short article. Broadly speaking, three principle strands of meaning have emerged. Happily for us, they indicate that 'daily bread' remains the best option for those of us who pray in English. The possible shades of meaning are:

> *Give us today our bread for today*
> *Give us today our bread day by day (or our bread for tomorrow)*
> *Give us today our bread for the future.*

As I pointed out in the previous article, 'bread' stands for 'food'. The first two suggestions, therefore, represent a down-to-earth, straightforward request to God for a sufficiency of food each day of our lives. The third suggestion is more spiritual. It is influenced by John's Gospel, chapter 6, in which Jesus refers to himself as "the bread of life". We are taught in the Old Testament (Deuteronomy 8.3) that "that man does not live on bread alone but on every word that comes from the mouth of the LORD." This teaching is strongly endorsed by Jesus (the Word made flesh) in John's Gospel as well as in the story of his temptations. So the bread "for the future" could be the Eucharistic bread in Holy Communion, our spiritual sustenance, food for eternal life. This approach begins to move away from pure translation and into the realm of interpretation.

My scholarly guide (***Ernst Lohmeyer: see article above***) who provided me with much of the substance of these two articles, suggests that Jesus might have deliberately used a rare Aramaic word to qualify the word "bread", simply in order to make his disciples reflect more deeply on the prayer and its meaning. His style of teaching (e.g. the use of parables) is often for this purpose.

---

[12]  There is a 5th century papyrus that includes the word 'epious'. This seems to be an abbreviation for a word that could mean 'daily ration' but there is no certainty.

## Challenge for today

Probably the most influential of Bible translators from Greek into English was William Tyndale. In his version of 1536 he translated *epiousios* as "daily". Practically all subsequent translators have followed his lead, and I am sure this is right. It is also right that we should linger in thought and prayer over each word in The Lord's Prayer and consider the possibility of deeper layers of meaning and interpretation. In my previous article I said that I was challenged when I prayed "give us today our daily bread" in the supermarket, while I was loading the trolley with the week's (not the day's) shopping. For I suddenly realised that my prayer could be interpreted quite differently from what I had thought. I was actually praying that God would put a limit on the stuff that I was buying: enough for the day, no more. And I found myself calling to mind the teaching of Jesus: "take no thought for the morrow", "do not be anxious about food", "do not store up treasure on earth", words from the same chapter (6) in Matthew's Gospel in which The Lord's Prayer occurs. At the same time, using the words "us" and "our", I was also praying for all of us shoppers with our loaded baskets, enjoying the privilege of being part of an affluent society that has got so used to a super-abundance of food and other goods that we have forgotten what it is like to be hungry. So this petition could perhaps be rendered: "Help us, Lord, not to overload our trolleys, larders, fridges and freezers with more than we need, and to be satisfied with a simple sufficiency needful for each day as it comes."

By way of a kind of postscript, I was intrigued to have discovered one popular modern version of the Bible in English that didn't use the word "daily". This was *The Message* by Eugene Patterson. His 'Bible' is admittedly a paraphrase, not a translation, and he renders the petition "give us this day our daily bread" as "Keep us alive with three square meals." I think he must be an American football player! In my praying I will stay with the traditional form, at the same time being rather glad that I did not live and pray in the 10<sup>th</sup> century, when "daily" (in Old English) was spelt *gedaegwhamlican*!

# Lead us not into temptation 1 …

*exploring an awkward bit of the world's best-known prayer.*
Solihull Parish Magazine April / May 2015

This is the sixth petition of the Lord's Prayer and surely the one that gives us the most difficulty. Personally, I am very content with the rest of the prayer, but this petition has challenged me for years. What does it mean? Why should God want to lead me into temptation? I confess that even now, I cannot find a totally satisfactory answer, but there are some pointers that can help us towards a fuller understanding.

To begin with, it is worth saying that this petition has been a problem for Bible commentators ever since the Gospels began to circulate at the end of the first century. From then until now, translators and interpreters have had a tendency to soften the wording, usually suggesting that it could mean: "do not allow us to be led into temptation". But that won't do. The Greek text in the Gospels of Matthew and Luke is clear and unambiguous, "do not lead (or bring) us into temptation" and we are left to wrestle with the meaning. I have three main pointers to share, two in this article and one in the next.

**1. The word "temptation".**
We commonly think of being tempted as being seduced, perhaps by another person or perhaps by the devil, to do something naughty. This touches the surface of the meaning. As children of God and followers of Jesus, we learn from our early years that we should resist what we know to be wrong. As mature Christian adults we can deepen our understanding and accept the idea that temptations can be regarded as tests of our moral fibre and of our Christian discipleship. Dealing with such tests can contribute towards our spiritual growth.

Some modern versions of the Lord's Prayer use the wording, "do not bring us to the time of trial", meaning the time of testing. This is a better translation, but we need to realise that the Greek word actually implies a far more serious situation than the common allurements to naughtiness that we meet in everyday life. It has the weighty sense of something really big and serious, of a test so severe as to pose a real threat, physical, mental, emotional and spiritual, to our equilibrium: a threat that could lead to disintegration of the self, body and soul.

The ultimate example of such a test is what happened to Jesus on Good Friday, but I don't want to expand on that here. It will be better for us to enlarge our understanding by considering carefully the temptations of Christ in the wilderness following his baptism. Significantly, Luke tells us that Jesus was "driven" (led, or brought) by the Spirit (of God) into this situation. We don't do justice to the story if we think that Jesus was simply playing word games with Satan. Those temptations, or tests, were aimed at the very foundations of his humanity. They came as the climax of years of spiritual reflection on his part, self-assessment regarding his status and his calling. At that level of testing, one becomes aware more than ever of the power of evil, and of the desperate need for God's grace to counteract it.

So when we pray "lead us not into temptation" we sometimes need to realise that this has reference to something really serious, to an event or circumstance that, actually or potentially, can threaten disintegration. And now it becomes clear why the sixth petition is immediately followed by the plea "deliver us from evil".

## 2. A Kingdom prayer.

We need to take notice that The Lord's Prayer is a Kingdom prayer. In Matthew's Gospel, it comes right in the middle of the three chapters (five, six and seven) that form the famous Sermon on the Mount. This is where Jesus sets out his programme or manifesto for the Kingdom of God. The Kingdom is mentioned twice in The Lord's Prayer. At the start it is the Kingdom which is still to come and for which we pray "thy Kingdom come". And at the end the tense changes to the present, "thine *is* the Kingdom", which signifies that, under the lordship of Jesus, the Kingdom is here and now, and we are already among its citizens. This reminds us that The Lord's Prayer is a community prayer, which we pray, not in isolation, but in company with all those who believe in and strive to follow Jesus as Lord.

Now let us understand that wherever and whenever the structures of conventional religion become hidebound and arthritic, the teaching of Jesus about God's Kingdom is radical, prophetic and generally uncomfortable. And in the context of worldly power structures that are oppressive and slanted in favour of the wealthy and successful, his

Kingdom teaching is actually subversive. This means that Jesus was at risk when he was teaching and proclaiming the Kingdom. It also means that all true citizens of God's Kingdom are also at risk. This, surely, is blindingly obvious in our own day, when Christians in some parts of the world are being persecuted to death, and where secular values in the developed nations are steadily undermining true faith in God, and ignoring or scorning the challenging teachings of the Gospel.

Consequently, praying "lead us not into temptation" becomes a vital plea for believers not to find themselves beyond the margins of the household of faith, where they are a prey to unbridled fraud and deceit, unchecked bodily appetites, overwhelming mockery and derision, and subjected to cruel and meaningless pain and despair.

In my second article in next month's magazine, I shall reveal my third pointer towards an understanding of this sixth petition of The Lord's Prayer. Then I hope to find the beginning of some sort of an answer to the still unanswered question as to why God could possibly want to lead us away from the Kingdom of Heaven to which we truly belong, and towards the realm of darkness and god-forsakenness where evil can abound.

———⟨○⟩———

# Lead us not into temptation 2

I have given two pointers towards a deeper understanding of this difficult text.

To recapitulate for a moment: We need to understand that The Lord's Prayer is a Kingdom prayer. The very first phrase is "Our Father" and not "My Father". However much we use and value the Lord's Prayer in private devotion, it is clearly given to us as a corporate and community prayer for the citizens of the Kingdom of God. We also have to realise that the word "temptation" has lost a good deal of its stronger meaning. Certainly, we can pray "lead us not into temptation" to help us address those moments when we are tempted or enticed to do something that is wrong and sinful. But the Greek word *peirasmos* is much more robust and serious. It carries the idea of a truly stressful time of testing, trial and challenge, as a steel girder may be tested to breaking point. During the early centuries of Christendom, the Church suffered persecution, and martyrdom was relatively commonplace. Christians must have been really fervent in praying that God would keep them away from the violent and painful testing of their faith at the hands of pagan authorities that would use them as blood sport for gladiators, or human bait for wild beasts.

### 3. An answered prayer.

My third pointer is quite simply to suggest that probably for most of us (and certainly for me personally), this sixth petition is an *already answered* prayer. The words "lead us not into temptation" can be taken as meaning "do not bring us to such a testing that we are overwhelmed and our faith is annihilated." Looking over my past life, I am enormously grateful that, at least up until now, testing such as this has never been my experience. By the grace of God, I have never had to face persecution, let alone martyrdom, for my beliefs, and it seems unlikely that I will have to face such trials in the future. On a less dramatic level of testing, as a youngster, I was taught to identify and confess my "besetting sins". Put like that, it sounds a bit grim and old-fashioned, but it is really good spiritual common sense to call to mind and prayerfully to regret those many occasions when I have given way to weakness.

Looking back over the years, I now realise, rather to my surprise, how often I seem to have been mysteriously led away from situations where I had been in danger of making a fool of myself by giving way to temptation. I have come to the conclusion that God is a kind of shock-absorber. When you are driving a modern car, you notice the big bumps and potholes, but because of the efficiency of the shock-absorbers you just don't realise how many small bumps and unevenesses happen in between. In a similar kind of way, God has not only attempted to warn me about the (spiritual) potholes and unfriendly drain covers, he also appears to have absorbed all kinds of sinful bumps and unevenesses along the way of life without my realising it. That can only mean that the prayer "lead us not into temptation" has been quietly answered as many times as it has been said.

One final word towards an answer to the question that I raised at the end of the previous article: why would God lead us into temptation (the time of testing)? This connects with the vexed question as to why there is so much suffering in the world. I doubt if there is a satisfactory answer to that, and if there is, it cannot be expressed in a few sentences. All I can do is to point to the Bible, which has sometimes been called "The Book of Temptations".

The God whom we meet in the Bible is the Supreme Being who engages with the human creation that he/she loves (please remember that God transcends gender, so when I write 'he', make any adjustment you wish). God is in continuous relationship with us, not as an autocrat, but rather as a good and loving parent. The 'family home', which is our world or universe, is continually created and re-created as an environment in which freedom can flourish. Such an environment cannot happen without an allowance being made for the existence of the shadow side. Nor can the children in such an environment achieve a mature and balanced adulthood without being made aware (often painfully) of this shadow side.

So when we pray to the Father, "lead us not into temptation", we are legitimately asking that we shall not be put into a position where our confrontation with darkness and evil would deprive us of all our sense of direction, purpose, love, hope and belonging.

That is by no means a complete answer to the problem of 'theodicy' which is the scholars' term for the problem of suffering, but it will suffice as a kind of end-note to my two articles which I hope will help towards a clearer understanding and appreciation of the sixth petition of our amazing Christian family prayer.

*(Note. In relation to this article, I strongly advise you to look up the following: Matthew 4. 1-11; Matthew 26. 36-41; Luke 22. 28-30; 1 Corinthians 10. 6-13; Hebrews 4. 14-16; James 1. 12-16; Revelation 3.10)*

**Witley Court**

This once-upon-a-time stately home is situated in North Worcestershire. It was destroyed by fire in 1937 and became a stately ruin. Happily for posterity it has been in the care of English Heritage since 1972. When I did this sketch, not much restoration work had been carried out. In more recent years, English Heritage has restored a substantial area of the beautiful gardens. Best of all, they have also restored the fountains, the biggest of which is in the foreground of my sketch. And they work! And they give a spectacular display on the hour for people's entertainment and delight.

In the background on the left is the church dedicated to St Michael & All Angels, with its elegant cupola. This was never a private chapel, but has always been the parish church for the villages of Great and Little Witley. During the 18th century, the owners of Witley Court built and lavishly adorned the church in the fashionable Italian style, probably replacing an older building. Successive owners continued to enhance the building during the 19th and early 20th centuries. After the fire in 1937, the church began to deteriorate, but in 1960 the parishioners formed a committee for its restoration. The skilful work of restoration continued in phases until its completion in 2016. Today, the glory of the interior with its wonderful Italian artwork can be appreciated by the general public whenever the church is open, which is quite often (check the website).

In its heyday in the Victorian era, Witley Court was owned by the Earl of Dudley. He occasionally invited his friend, the Prince of Wales (later to become King Edward VII), for a house party.

# Acknowledgements

I must begin by saying thank you, first to the editors and readers of the Solihull Parish Magazine – to the editors for including my contributions to their *Faith Matters* pages, and to those readers who have read what I have written, made interesting comments, and suggested that some of the articles might be collected into a book some day. To you, I say "thank you, and here it is".

A big thank you to my two dear daughters, Naomi and Rachel. Naomi very kindly read the book in draft, launched a raft of sensible amendments and suggestions, and has given me lots of encouragement. She also wrote the blurb that appears on the back cover. Rachel happens to be, amongst other things, an experienced proofreader. I am equally grateful to her for having applied her skills to my text and made all kinds of useful comments. Any errors or oddities, real or apparent, that remain are entirely my own responsibility.

A final word of thanks to *The Choir Press* who have helpfully dealt with all the mysteries and technicalities of self-publishing which are far beyond my understanding.

# *The Author*

Robert Burns famously wrote: "O wad some Power the giftie gie us, to see oursels as ithers see us!" Or, in modern English, "Oh would some Power the gift give us, to see ourselves as others see us." I am quite sure that to see ourselves as others see us is an excellent thing to do, so much more sensible than any attempt we make at self-aggrandisement, or, to put it bluntly, showing off. Be that as it may, this little part of my book is "me as I see me" so I will make it very brief.

In 2011, I went to a drawing class for a refresher. One of the exercises was to do a self-portrait, and this was the result. It is a bit alarming, I know, and of course it's a mirror image, so I am really the other way round: for instance, I part my hair on the other side in real life. Be that as it may, I think it will be sensible to add a recent photo to let you know how the camera sees me:

Just to complete the picture, I'm nearer ninety than eighty, live in Solihull, England, am married with three children, two grandchildren and three great-grandchildren. I retired from active ordained ministry in the Church of England in 1998. I started playing the piano before I could talk, and still play when I've finished talking. I also like reading books and have written, co-authored or edited nine books including this one. And I don't have a television set.

# WHITBY ABBEY

Illustration on the back cover

The watercolour sketch on the back cover is the only illustration in the book that was not done by me. I include it simply because of the strong sentimental association that I have with it. It was painted by my mother, Monica, when she was expecting her sixth child: you've guessed it . . . me! She told me (later, of course) that she was enraptured by the sunset display enlightening the abbey ruins. She showed me in her sketchbook the initial drawing she had made on site with pencilled notes about the colours, so that she could complete the picture when she got home. I guess that she must have been sitting near the place where, in more recent years, a new road bridge was built across the river Esk.

The picture now hangs above my desk. Beside it is another watercolour, one which I did 70 years later. It is not included, partly because it lacks the flair that my mother's picture has, and partly because it was not sketched on site, but copied from a book about Yorkshire. The viewpoint is Sandsend which is a couple of miles away from Whitby, and the abbey is only just visible on the horizon.

Below both pictures is a small plaque from a London East-End pub. The hostelry is situated on the North bank of the River Thames and oddly named *The Prospect of Whitby*. Apparently a small ship of that name used to dock close by when the pub was rebuilt early in the 19th century. It was a collier bringing coals **from** (not to) Newcastle, which reminds me straight away of the poem I learnt at school, "Cargoes" by John Masefield. After the "quinquireme from Niniveh" and the "stately Spanish galleon" with their precious and beautiful cargoes comes the third verse:

> *Dirty British coaster with a salt-caked smoke stack,*
> *Butting through the Channel in the mad March days,*
> *With a cargo of Tyne coal,*
> *Road-rails, pig-lead,*
> *Firewood, iron-ware, and cheap tin trays.*

The pub has a colourful history. It is worth looking it up on the Internet.